Letters to a Fellow Seeker

A SHORT INTRODUCTION TO THE QUAKER WAY

by

Steve Chase

QUAKERPRESS PHILADELPHIA, PA

LETTERS TO A FELLOW SEEKER

Printed in the United States of America

Composition and design by David Botwinik
Cover photograph by David Botwinik

ISBN 978-1-937768-02-7 (paperback)
        978-1-937768-03-4 (digital)

Library of Congress Cataloging-in-Publication Data
Chase, Steve.
        Letters to a fellow seeker : a short introduction to the Quaker way /
by Steve Chase.
        p. cm.
        ISBN 978-1-937768-02-7 (soft cover) -- ISBN 978-1-937768-03-4 (epub)
        1. Society of Friends—Correspondence. I. Title.
BX7731.3.C27 2012
289.6—dc23
                                2012017257

To order more copies of this publication or other Quaker titles call
1-800-966-4556 or see the online catalog at www.quakerbooks.org.

Contents

An Introduction

We believe that every person is loved by the Divine Spirit. There are Quakers of all ages, religious backgrounds, races, education, sexual orientations, gender identities, and classes. ... You are welcome to join us as you are.

— *Friends General Conference's Newcomers Card*

Dear Reader,

Welcome to this short book on the simple, radical, and contemporary spiritual path of Quakers, a group more formally referred to as the Religious Society of Friends, or Friends for short. My hope is that my personal stories and reflections about being a Quaker will help you imagine what it may be like to be an active participant in the Religious Society of Friends today, and perhaps even consider whether the Quaker way might be a meaningful spiritual path for you. At the very least, I hope this book will answer some of your questions about the Quaker movement and lead to a better understanding of this unusual spiritual tradition.

As a long-time spiritual seeker myself, I would like to start by sharing my own motivations for exploring the Quaker movement over forty years ago. You may have other reasons for exploring the Quaker way, but these are the four that still move me. First, I have long sought to directly experience divine love, presence, and guidance in my life, even when I didn't quite have words to describe this inward yearning. Second, in my deepest heart of hearts, I have long felt the call to foster a more spiritually fulfilling, socially just, and ecologically sustainable human presence on this planet. Third, I have wanted to stay faithful to the compassionate and nonviolent path of Jesus, Mohandas Gandhi, and Martin Luther King, while working toward these goals. Fourth, I have long felt that it would be beneficial to not "go it alone," but to lay down spiritual roots in the rich soil of a vibrant faith community that offers inspiration, challenge, discovery, common ground, fellowship, and profound spiritual openness.

While reading this book, I ask you to imagine that we are not strangers, but that we are old acquaintances who have not seen each other in a long time, and that we recently crossed paths at a train station while each of us was waiting for our different connections home. Imagine that during this chance meeting, we sat down together, shot right past the small talk, and had a brief, but remarkably intimate talk about spirituality. Imagine then that this talk sparked the desire for more communication between us. Now imagine that instead of conventional chapters, this book is a collection of seven personal letters I have written to you responding to our train station conversation and to the letters you have written to me since, asking several questions about my spiritual experience as a Quaker and expressing some of your own yearnings and experiences as a spiritual seeker.

I invite you to make this imaginary leap with me as a way to enhance the tone of storytelling and intimate conversation in the pages that follow. My hope is that by sharing my personal stories and reflections in this intimate way, I will be able to offer a useful glimpse into the Quaker movement's spiritual faith and practice. My understanding of this religious path has deepened over the four decades since I first discovered that the Quaker movement exists and that it is a far more radical and contemporary spiritual path than suggested by the big picture of the funny looking man with an old black hat on Quaker Oats boxes. My hope is that some of my experience will be useful to you.

The topics covered in these "letters" include my own journey to the Quaker movement, how the Quaker way is related to the Christian faith, how I experience and understand the nature of Quaker worship, how we minister one to another in spiritual community, and how I and others try to practice our faith in the wider world as we seek to foster what Martin Luther King called "the Beloved Community." To offer a more complete perspective, the sixth letter discusses our struggles to be faithful in our personal lives, spiritual communities, and the wider world, and how we still all too often conform to this world and "miss the mark," which is the literal translation of the Hebrew word for sin. Finally, in my closing letter, I invite you to consider becoming a participant in the Quaker community. The story after that is unfinished. I hope that these "personal letters" will hold some real spiritual value for you wherever your spiritual journey takes you.

While I firmly believe that the Quaker way is not the only faith tradition of deep value, it is my experience that by following the Quaker way I am often able to touch a deep spiritual reality in my daily life. This is a source of both guidance and grace for me, one that offers a soulful alternative to both hard-edged, modern secularism on the one hand and dogmatic religious fundamentalism on the other. If this spiritual middle path intrigues you, I hope you will read the rest of this short book and consider attending a Quaker meeting for worship in your area.

In the Spirit,
Steve Chase

P.S. You might be wondering about where the words "Quaker" and "Friend" come from and if they are interchangable. The term "Friend" in the name of the Religious Society of Friends was picked up from a story in the gospel of John where Jesus is recorded as saying to his followers that they are no longer merely his students or disciples, but they are now his friends. The word "Quaker," however, was originally a derogatory slang term used by critics to insult and belittle Friends. As far as anybody can tell, the term "Quaker" was first used in 1650 by Gervase Bennet, an English judge who thought the Friends movement was heretical. Friends increasingly started describing themselves as Quakers, since the term was widely known. Both terms are now used interchangeably. In the letters that follow, I mostly use the word Quaker, which I think is still better known, but I could just as easily have used the word Friend throughout.

LETTER 1

My Journey to the Quaker Movement

Dear Pat,

It was great to bump into you last week at Union Station in DC. What a fun surprise after all these years. I also loved our talk. As brief as it was, I was touched by how quickly we started speaking about the deeper spiritual concerns and yearnings in our hearts these days. I am very happy to answer your questions about the Quaker movement, which has been my primary spiritual home for over forty years now.

To begin, let me share a little about how I first started attending Quaker meeting as a teenager. I was not born into a Quaker family. As a child, I sometimes attended local Episcopal church services with my mom, and I also occasionally went to other churches and synagogues with various friends and neighbors. None of these religious services or communities ever fully engaged me, however. My strongest spiritual identity growing up was as a Scout. You may laugh, but for many years the Cub Scouts and the Boy Scouts were the closest things I had to an ongoing spiritual community.

I loved the weekly Scout meetings, the simple rituals, the service projects in between meetings, the time spent camping outdoors, and the regular fellowship and fun I had with other Scouts and with the volunteer Scout leaders who guided us. I also loved how the Boy Scouts had core values that mattered to me. Being a Scout meant that I had pledged to be trustworthy, helpful, friendly, courteous, kind, thrifty, brave, moral, and reverent. It also meant doing my duty to God and country. Those were things I took very seriously and still do.

By 1968 I was 13 and, through my mother's encouragement, I had already found a model in Martin Luther King Jr. with his call for a nonviolent revolution to end racism, materialism, and militarism in our nation. As I saw it, my duty to God and country was to help our nation become what King called a "Beloved Community" of peace, justice, and equality. It turned out that my scoutmaster did not see it that way.

Our difference of opinion came to a head one hot summer day when our troop was in the town square of Galesburg, Illinois, for our annual Boy Scout Jamboree. As I finished my scheduled tasks that morning, I noticed a small, silent peace vigil at the edge of the square with folks holding up signs opposing the ongoing U.S. invasion and occupation of Vietnam. I had never before seen anyone stand up against the war in my town and I was torn. I wanted to join them, yet I also felt some fear and hesitation about walking over and taking a public stand smack dab in the middle of my town.

In that moment of indecision, I thought of King's daring speech at the Riverside Church on April 4, 1967. In that fateful speech, which I heard about from my college age brother, King first voiced in public his opposition to this unjust war. He called on all hesitant people to follow him now and end their own silence about the war. Given that King was my hero, I decided to follow his example on that hot summer day in Galesburg. So, I screwed up my courage to walk across the town square and join the silent peace vigil. It was my first overt act of social activism and I was glad to have taken this step. I was no longer just admiring King. I was following him. This felt good and right to me.

My sense of inner peace was short lived, though. Almost instantly, my scoutmaster spotted me standing in my uniform as part of this silent peace vigil, and he was furious. He ran over, grabbed me, and physically dragged me out of the vigil line. He started shaking me by the shoulders and yelling at me that I was a "communist," a "traitor," and a "disgrace to the Boy Scout uniform." He shouted that I was no longer welcome in his troop and that he would make sure no other troop in town would ever let me join. He then abruptly pushed me away and stormed off. I don't think now that his action represented the views of the leadership of the Boy Scouts of America, but I had no way to know that then. I stood there stunned and abandoned. Blessedly, an elderly woman from the vigil came up to me, put her hand on my arm, and said, "Young man, I'm sorry that happened to you. Just know that you will always be welcome at a Quaker Meeting."

At home, later that same day, I asked my mom about the Quakers and she shared with me what she knew about the Religious Society of Friends. She also told me that as much as my dad disapproved of religion, he was a financial contributor to the American Friends Service Committee. She said he admired both their peace advocacy and their international relief work. My mom also said that it would be fine with her if I wanted to attend a Quaker "meeting for worship" instead of going with her to our regular church services the next day.

Later that night, I worked up my courage for the second time that day and called the number in the phone book under the listing "Galesburg Friends Meeting (Quakers)." I was touched that the woman who answered the phone was as welcoming as the woman at the vigil—even though I was a 13-year-old kid! I asked her where and when they held their services and what to expect. She gave me the address and said that the Quakers in Galesburg sat silently in a circle expectantly waiting to be touched and guided by the Spirit of God, which many of them often called the Seed, the Light Within, the Inward Christ, or the Inward Teacher.

This woman also said that their worship started when the first person sat down in the room and "centered down" into silence. The rest of the worshipers joined this person in silence until all were assembled. She added that if anyone felt moved by the Spirit during the meeting they would stand up and offer a vocal message or a song to the whole group and then sit back down and the group would return to silence. She said there was no pastor or priest, and anyone could be moved to give ministry, including men, women, and children. I had never heard of a worship service like this before and I loved the sound of it.

I also asked this woman what do Quakers believe. She answered that the core Quaker belief was that every man, woman, and child on this planet has the spiritual capacity to directly experience God's love, presence, and guidance in their lives and that if we open our hearts to this sacred Light Within it can transform our personal lives, our families, our communities, and our world. She said that over three hundred years experience of attending to the Light Within had taught Quakers the value of encouraging each other to lead lives of integrity, simplicity, equality, compassion, stewardship, and community activism for peace and social justice. She called these the "Quaker testimonies." I loved that answer, too.

Well, the next day I went to my first Quaker meeting for worship with a group of seventeen or so Galesburg Quakers. We sat together in a big living room belonging to one of the local members. It was odd at first, but I found it both challenging and exhilarating to sit quietly in the deepening silence, open to the touch of Divine Presence. Sure, my mind wandered a bit, and I was not really sure what I was "supposed" to be doing, but pretty soon I actually felt something happening inside of me that I had never experienced in any religious service before.

I felt actively engaged in deep spiritual seeking and sometime during that very first meeting for worship—and many times since—I felt as if I was directly breathing Spirit in and out, directly breathing compassion and wisdom in and out, directly breathing love and justice in and out. This experience was immediate and powerful. I was not just thinking about what other people in the past had said about God or religion. Instead, I felt profoundly moved by glimmers of direct connection and attunement to the Spirit, the Inward Teacher that the woman on the phone had mentioned.

As we all sat together in the prayerful silence, a few worshipers also stood up at different times and offered brief spoken ministry. I particularly remember that the woman who talked to me at the peace vigil spoke haltingly, but movingly, about how the call to nonviolently defend the Vietnamese people from our government's violence was an outward expression of our deep inner faith as Quakers. She felt it was God's will that all the faithful in our country should take up this task even more strongly than we had to date. I felt particularly stirred by her heartfelt ministry and loved the fact that in the Quaker movement women were encouraged to be ministers. I knew my mom would approve.

After a little over an hour of silence and short vocal ministry, the Galesburg Quakers closed their meeting for worship by shaking hands. I was welcomed as a newcomer and one person, who described himself as the clerk of the meeting, made a few announcements. We then got up and talked informally over snacks in the dining room. Somebody mentioned to me that not all Quakers met in people's houses and that most Quaker meetings around the world had built simple meeting houses for their congregations. Another woman spoke up and said that she had worshipped both in meeting houses and living rooms, and she most enjoyed the intimacy of the small "house meetings." Another Quaker said her favorite meetings for worship were the ones she had attended that were held outdoors.

I asked my new acquaintances if there was anything I could read to learn more about the Quaker movement. One man took me to the meeting's "library," which was a couple of shelves in the living room. He pulled out a copy of a book called *Faith and Practice*. He explained that it was an anthology of many different statements about the Quaker movement written by different Quakers throughout history and that it also included a lot of recent material about Quaker practice written by a committee of the Illinois Yearly Meeting, the regional association of Quakers that included the Galesburg Friends Meeting. He explained that most yearly meetings around the world create their own guidebooks, which are reviewed and updated every twenty to thirty years as part of a spiritual consensus-building process within each yearly meeting. As he put it, "We believe in continuing revelation."

While reading this book at home later, I found a particularly interesting section called "Advices and Queries," which included a list of questions designed to help Quakers think more deeply about their own day-to-day faith and practice. It addressed personal conduct, home and family, environmental stewardship, vocational choices, social responsibility and community engagement, and peace and reconciliation. It also addressed how we prepare for meeting for worship and how we engage in the spiritual life of the meeting community. To me, all these questions seemed like some of the most important questions we could possibly ask ourselves.

The "Advices and Queries" also included a set of questions about personal spiritual life that went something like the passage below, which is taken from my current yearly meeting's book of *Faith and Practice*:

> Do you live in thankful awareness of God's constant presence in your life? Are you sensitive and obedient to leadings of the Holy Spirit? Do you seek to follow Jesus, who shows us the way? Do you nurture your spiritual life with prayer and silent

waiting and with regular study of the Bible and other devotional literature?

Now, I did not yet know what my own answers to these questions were, but I was intrigued about reflecting on each of them as part of my spiritual journey.

I was particularly struck by the query about following Jesus. I had always thought that being a Christian meant believing a specific set of doctrinal beliefs about Jesus so you could go to heaven after you died. But all these Quaker questions focused on our lives here and now, and none of them mentioned any specific belief that you had to hold about Jesus to be a Quaker, except that his life "shows us the way" and it is wise to follow in his footsteps.

Just a few days earlier, I had followed in Martin Luther King's footsteps, and King, in turn, was certainly following in the footsteps of Jesus in his work for peace and justice. I now felt somehow closer to the source of something wonderful and powerful, something I could read and think about, but also something I could now directly experience, just as I seemed to do in my very first Quaker meeting for worship.

While there was much more to think about and to learn, of course, I already knew that I loved the experience of Quaker worship, of sitting in silence with other seekers trying to be open to wonder, possibility, love, challenge, guidance, and deep inner peace. Returning to this little band of Galesburg Quakers each week for group worship was a spiritual practice that nourished and excited me. A couple of years later, when I read a book by Robert Barclay, an early British Quaker theologian, I found that people had been having experiences like mine for over three hundred years. As Barclay put it:

When I came into the silent assemblies of God's people, I felt a secret power among them, which touched my heart, and as I gave way unto it, I found the evil weakening in me, and the good raised up, and so I became thus knit and united unto them, hungering more and more after the increase of this power and life, whereby I might feel myself perfectly redeemed.

While I might have said it a little differently in 1968, my first experience of Quaker worship was astonishingly similar to Barclay's.

I now look back on my first Quaker meeting for worship with deep gratitude. It felt like coming home. This, I said to myself early on, is my spiritual community and this is my spiritual path. Today, as a member of the Putney Friends Meeting in Vermont, I still feel the same. In my decades of participating in silent Quaker worship, I have found that it is often possible for those present to become aware of a divine love and spiritual fullness that far transcends ordinary existence. This sense of living communion, in turn, has a way of healing, transforming, and guiding our daily lives.

The intimacy, openness, and mutual responsibility of our way of worship also influences our character as a spiritual community. We regularly come together for more than meeting for worship, as powerful and as central as that is in our spiritual lives. For example, at Putney Friends Meeting, we describe ourselves on our website as "a Quaker congregation that meets in Putney, Vermont, for worship, fellowship, education, and activist support."

We eat potlucks together, delight in our kids, offer them creative religious education, have intimate conversations that matter, share our faith journeys, read and discuss books together, watch movies or bring in speakers, organize healing circles, go together to larger Quaker gatherings, and some of us join nonviolent action trainings to prepare to commit civil disobedience in an attempt the support the State of Vermont to close an aging and leaking nuclear reactor nearby. We cry and laugh together, share our joys and concerns, rent out our meeting house at very low rates to a network of home schoolers and AA groups, and at our business meetings, we discuss if, when, and how we should put solar panels on our meeting house roof.

Quaker congregations like Putney Friends Meeting are participatory, volunteer-run, spiritual communities led by committees and coordinated by rotating officers as well as by our monthly business meetings. These meetings are open to the entire community and are held to discern together the will of God in our affairs. Our decisions reflect a spiritual unity that we can all acknowledge, rather than a count of votes. This radical approach to "church government" is very common in the Quaker movement. Ours is a first-hand, do-it-yourself faith community. This is something I have long treasured about the Quaker way.

I hope this helps answer your question about how and why I began my spiritual journey to the Quaker movement. Is there anything else you are wondering about? Does any of this resonate with you?

Affectionately,
Steve

LETTER 2

Are Quakers Christians?

Dear Pat,

Thanks for writing back so quickly. I'm glad you found the story about my becoming a Quaker useful. I am also glad that you found it funny in places and inspiring in others. I particularly think your follow-up question about whether Quakers are Christians is an important one to explore.

Let me start addressing your question by offering a little historical perspective. The Quaker movement arose in the mid-1600s during the English Civil War. During that turbulent time, many people were looking to revive a "primitive Christianity" untainted by what they saw as the "imperial" distortions that had come to dominate Christendom in their day. The emerging Quaker faith and practice in this period was deeply rooted in both prophetic Judaism and the radical spiritual renewal movement led by Jesus in first century Palestine. Quakers also believed that it was now time to be directly led by the indwelling Spirit of God that had so inspired and guided Jesus during his lifetime and ministry. The early Quakers invited all people to turn to this Inward Teacher. They structured their worship so that it would be conducted as simple silent waiting on the Spirit without priests or any outward sacraments, symbols, or rituals.

At this point, the early Quaker movement was just a rag-tag band of English farmers, domestic workers, laborers, tradespeople, small business owners, and a handful of academics and a few renegades from the English nobility. They met outside in fields, or in pubs, barns, or private homes. One thing that held these spiritual rebels together was that they, like Jesus, felt directly called by the Spirit of God to reject the dominant values of their day, which treasured power, wealth, and privilege, and to act instead to bring forth a renewed social world that was simple, just, peaceful, and sustainable.

Not surprisingly, the early Quakers were considered a significant threat to the status quo, a fact that I have long appreciated about my spiritual ancestors. I like the idea of there being lots of "dangerous Quakers" everywhere! The early Quakers were intensely persecuted by the English government and were repeatedly called heretics, heathens, and blasphemers by judges, priests, and even violent mobs. Many Quakers were jailed and some of them died from the harsh conditions in jail. Many conventional church leaders of the day denied that Quakers were Christian in any way. So, clearly, the question of whether or not Quakers are Christians has been a controversial one for centuries. The answer depends in large part on who you ask.

OK, so now let's zoom forward in time to 1968, just as I was trying to find my own answer to your important question. A few weeks after I first read that set of *Faith and Practice* queries about spiritual life, which I mentioned in my last letter, I asked one of the older Galesburg Quakers about what it meant that Quakers seemed to put their main emphasis on following Jesus rather than on believing the many specific claims about him that most people felt were essential in order to be a Christian.

This guy laughed and said that he had read the Bible several times and noticed that whenever Jesus was asked about how to live a faithful spiritual life, he never answered, "You must believe that my mother is a virgin and I am God." Instead, my new friend said, Jesus would answer all such questions with such teachings as "be loving, as God is loving." For this man, following the way of Jesus was the very essence of the Quaker movement, which he described as a spiritual community that encourages its members to live Spirit-led lives of simplicity, integrity, equality, nonviolence, community involvement, and unity with nature. I was touched and inspired by this conversation.

My new mentor also explained to me that there are three kinds of loving talked about in the Jewish and Christian scriptures that have always been important to the Quaker movement: loving the Spirit of God with all one's heart and strength; loving our neighbors, including our enemies, as ourselves; and loving and caring for God's good earth. This, he added, is the prophetic Jewish wisdom that Jesus taught and embodied in his own life and ministry.

This is also the teaching of George Fox, one of the early English leaders of the Religious Society of Friends. As my new mentor showed me, these three forms of faithful loving were spelled out right on page two of Fox's journal. As someone raised by my dad to love wilderness and the natural world, I was particularly struck that as far back as the 1600s Quakers were talking about loving the "unity of creation" and urging people to avoid "devouring the creation" in violation of "the covenant of life." I read George Fox's words on this subject two years before the first Earth Day and I was again impressed and moved.

These conversations, and some of the vocal ministry in the meetings for worship I attended, finally inspired me to read the gospels of Matthew, Mark, Luke, and John myself, as well as the preserved letters of some of the early organizers of the spiritual movement led by Jesus. Frankly, I think it is interesting that none of these people ever used the words "Christian" or "Christianity" to describe themselves or their faith. They simply called their spiritual movement "The Way of God," or "The Way" for short.

I also have to admit that while reading the Bible for the first time in 1968, I was a bit surprised by the depth of spiritual wisdom and the intense hunger for justice that I found in the life and ministry of Jesus. I was expecting to find the static, apolitical Jesus, concerned only about the afterlife, that I had mostly heard about in church. I could now see why Martin Luther King was so drawn to Jesus as his guide and savior, something I didn't fully understand before.

I certainly had never known, for example, that in his first public act of ministry, Jesus echoed the words of the prophet Isaiah (61:1–2) and said to the other worshipers in his synagogue:

> The Spirit of the Lord is upon me,
> because he has anointed me to preach good news to the poor.
> He has sent me to proclaim release to the captives
> and recovering of sight to the blind,
> to set at liberty those who are oppressed,
> to proclaim the acceptable year of the Lord.

While reading this, I experienced these words as if someone stood up in the silence of a meeting for worship and gave inspired vocal ministry that went straight to my heart. I came to love Jesus intensely, and through him I felt closer to the Spirit that he had turned to so powerfully for divine presence, love, and guidance.

Later on, I also read the prophets in the Hebrew scriptures and found several spiritual ancestors there as well. I especially loved the Jewish feminine imagery of Sophia to signify the Inward Teacher, the spirit of divine wisdom that is accessible to all, something that Quaker theologian Robert Barclay also pointed to in 1692. I found it both strange and exhilarating to feel so connected to a living, pulsing spiritual tradition with ancient roots that spoke so powerfully to me across time. I was both comforted and challenged when I finally learned about Jesus and the prophets by reading the Bible myself, not just hearing about them from others.

As I kept going to meetings for worship, reading more, and talking with the Galesburg Quakers and then with the Quakers from DeKalb, Illinois, where I moved two years later, I increasingly felt that I was also kin with the earliest Quakers. They became my closest spiritual ancestors. Here was a radical spiritual renewal movement that embraced the nonviolent revolutionary path of Jesus. Three hundred years before me, these people had offered a liberating alternative to the idolatry and worship of dogma, wealth, hierarchy, war, and empire, which had come to dominate all the kingdoms in Europe as well as their state-sponsored churches. When I looked around me at the world I lived in during the late 1960s, filled with materialism and militarism at home and abroad, it still seemed to me that "primitive Christianity" needed to be revived and practiced in our world and in my own heart.

I could now answer all the *Faith and Practice* queries about spiritual life in the affirmative. Yes, I seek to live in thankful awareness of God's constant presence. Yes, I seek to be sensitive and obedient to leadings of the Holy Spirit. Yes, I seek to be a friend and follower of Jesus. And, yes, I seek to nurture my spiritual life with prayer, silent waiting worship, and regular study of the Bible and other spiritual literature. Taken together, this is a core part of what the Quaker way means to me.

But does this make me a Christian in today's world? Personally, I usually answer yes when asked, but it all depends on how people define the word. For example, back when I was fifteen and had been a practicing Quaker for about two years, I once fell into a conversation with an elderly street evangelist on the main street of DeKalb. He started our conversation by walking up to me, handing me a brochure, and asking, "Are you a Christian?"

As a teenage Quaker inspired by the Spirit of God and the prophetic ministry and life example of Jesus, I quickly answered yes. Yet, this man was not convinced at all and began asking many questions about my religious beliefs. After just a few minutes, he informed me that I was not a "true" Christian, even though I professed to be. As he explained it, I simply did not fit any meaningful definition of a Christian because my personal interpretations of God, Jesus, and the Bible were all wrong. In fact, he said I was worse off than someone who had never heard of Jesus Christ. I was a heretic.

For a brief moment, I tensed up, remembering how early Quakers were regularly condemned, beaten, and imprisoned on charges of heresy by the "orthodox" Christian authorities of their day. Yet, this situation was very different. The sincere gentleman in front of me was not an authority, nor did he wish to imprison me or harm me in any way. He simply wanted to convince me of the error of my ways. I could respect that.

No longer feeling threatened, I relaxed and became interested in the man's religious beliefs. I asked him what he thought it would take for me to become a "true" Christian. He replied that at a minimum a real Christian ascribes to particular articles of faith, for example, that Jesus is the only begotten son of God, that he is part of a three-person Godhead, that he sacrificed himself for the atonement of our sins, and that he rose bodily from the grave three days after his execution and will come again on a final Judgment Day. The evangelist also told me that all "non-believers," no matter how morally exemplary their lives, would be barred from heaven and would suffer eternal damnation in hell after their deaths.

I could now see why he did not think I was a Christian. This was not how I understood my own faith and practice at all. Certainly, the people in my Quaker meeting did not think that these intellectual notions about Jesus were essential for people to live in harmony with the Spirit, our neighbors, and the wider world of life. This was even true of those Quakers who did accept some of these beliefs, as some Quakers do.

While I don't know about you, as a fifteen-year-old Quaker back in 1970, I was far more concerned with living faithfully in the here and now than in worrying about a possible next life. I was also far less interested in people's theological beliefs about

Jesus than in our collectively figuring out how to follow Jesus's way of living in our own lives and times—to love God with all one's heart, strength, and soul; to love and care for one's neighbors as one's self; and to love God's good earth and all other forms of life. If people could help each other follow Jesus's transforming, Spirit-led way of life, regardless of their different theological beliefs about his status in the grand scheme of things, I was convinced that deep spiritual renewal was possible in our world.

I soon discovered that my new acquaintance had another standard for sorting out who was a "true" Christian from all those who professed to be. He said that for me to become a real Christian, I would also need to believe that every passage of the Bible is historically and factually accurate, as well as a complete, infallible revelation of God's will in all moral and doctrinal matters. As my yearly meeting's *Faith and Practice* notes, "Compiled from the inspiration of many ancient writers, the Bible has been for Friends not a blueprint or final authority, but a source of knowledge of God's ways with us." Viewing the Bible as a beloved and special source of spiritual wisdom and moral guidance was clearly not enough for my new street evangelist acquaintance.

He and I did agree about one thing, though. We both felt that the Spirit of God seeks out those of us who are lost in order to save us. Yet, even here, we soon found that we had very different views about what the word salvation means. For him, it seemed to mean an eternal afterlife in paradise if you accepted some very specific beliefs about God, Jesus, and the Bible. The Quakers I knew had a very different understanding of salvation. As Samuel Caldwell, the former general secretary of Philadelphia Yearly Meeting, beautifully says about the Quaker view of salvation:

Historically, it is this: God gives to every human being who comes into the world a measure of the Spirit through which divine guidance is inwardly received and the conscience enlightened. Every human being has direct access through this "inner Light" to divine inspiration for guidance for living in accordance with God's will. Those who discern and heed the promptings of this Inner Light in their daily lives are "saved"—that is, they come into fullness and wholeness of life and right relationship with God and one another. Those who resist, ignore, or disobey this Inner Light, even if they profess religion, are "damned"—that is, doomed to unhappiness and alienation from God, from themselves, and from one another.

I finally told the man that while I appreciated his strong convictions, I could not share them. Nor could I agree with his definition of a "true" Christian. I told him that I agreed instead with William Penn when he said, "To be like Christ then, is to be a Christian." I walked away not wanting to upset this man, but neither was I willing to abandon all of Christianity to him. The Quaker movement has long been a profound affirmation of following the mystical and prophetic faith and practice of Jesus of Nazareth and the spiritual renewal movement he led in first century Palestine. The challenge for us is in finding meaningful ways to understand and express this spiritual path in our contemporary world.

Now some easily identify this approach as Christian, as I do. Modern Quaker writer Phillip Gully also sees Quaker faith and practice as Christian, at least at its best. In his book *If the Church Were Christian: Rediscovering the Values of Jesus,* his chapter themes describe the core elements that he believes make a spiritual community a Christian community. For such communities:

○ Jesus is a model for living rather than an object of worship;

○ Affirming our potential is more important than condemning our brokenness;

○ Reconciliation is valued over judgment;

○ Gracious behavior is more important than right belief;

- Inviting questions is valued more than supplying answers;
- Encouraging personal exploration is more important than communal uniformity;
- Meeting human needs is more important than maintaining institutions;
- Peace is more important than power;
- Love is more important than sex; and
- Life is more important than the afterlife.

If this is how you also understand Christianity, then I think it is quite fair to call Quakers Christian.

At the same time, it is also important to know that Quakers have long been interfaith "universalists," as well as Christians. For example, here is a beautiful statement from colonial American Quaker John Woolman. I love its expansive and inclusive vision of faithfulness and salvation.

> There is a principle that is pure, placed in the human mind, which in different places and ages has had different names. It is, however, pure and proceeds from God. It is deep and inward, confined to no forms of religion nor excluded from any, where the heart stands in perfect sincerity. In whomsoever this takes root and grows, of what nation soever they become brethren in the best sense of the expression.

This is a remarkably radical way to understand the essence of the Quaker faith, and it raises the possibility of deep spiritual community and faithful unity reaching across the boundaries of nationalities, cultures, and even historic faith traditions. Even to the degree that you and I may both agree that Quakers are Christian, we are not exclusively so. Quakers believe that everyone who sincerely follows the Inward Teacher, regardless of their religion or culture, should be considered our spiritual brothers and sisters.

Today, our Quaker meetings often reflect this universalist value by the religious diversity of our communities. Some contemporary Quakers identify themselves as Jewish Quakers, Sufi Quakers, Buddhist Quakers, Hindu Quakers, Pagan Quakers, and a variety of other hybrid religious identities. This interesting mix of faithful unity and theological diversity is certainly the case at my own meeting. Yet, at its best, the non-Christian Quakers in our meetings draw from these other faith traditions qualities that are spiritually enlightening and fully consistent with following the way of Jesus and with the longstanding spiritual path of the Quaker movement. Gandhi, for example, was a far more faithful friend and follower of Jesus than many Christians, and he was Hindu. I would happily worship with him!

So here are my questions to you. Does this inclusive and somewhat fuzzy approach of the contemporary Quaker movement sound a little crazy to you? Or, do you see value in the Quaker movement today being a simple, radical, and contemporary faith tradition rooted in the best of Judaism and Christianity, open to new Light, and very appreciative of the complementary truths and practices that are found in many other spiritual traditions around the world? I truly won't be offended either way you answer. I'm just interested.

I have a cousin who lives in Arkansas and is a Southern Baptist. Like me, she also does her best to be loving and faithful in following the way of Jesus. We are both Jesus-inspired, Bible-reading, and Spirit-led Christians. Yet, she holds a more orthodox theology than I do about Jesus and thinks the Quaker movement is a little "crackers" because of our looser theological boundaries about who is welcomed into our communities and our meetings for worship. She loves me, sees my spiritual sincerity, but she does not see my version of Christianity as sufficient for eternal salvation.

My Quaker meeting would not feel like a good spiritual home for my cousin. She would feel uncomfortable worshipping regularly in a religious congregation where not everyone believed that Jesus is "the only begotten Son of God," or shared other "orthodox" beliefs that are very important to her.

If you agree with my cousin, I would be happy to provide some information about another stream of the Quaker movement that includes formally appointed pastors, planned worship services, and a greater reliance on orthodox Protestant Christian beliefs in their religious life. This stream of the Quaker movement, which began in the United States, has grown considerably since the nineteenth century. It has organized over a dozen yearly meetings in North America, has set up overseas missions, and has developed national and international networks, including Friends United Meeting and Evangelical Friends Church International. The majority of Quakers in Palestine, Kenya, Cuba, and several South American countries are part of this branch of the movement.

Quakers from what we call the "pastoral" or "programmed" tradition are dear spiritual siblings, and I have great respect for their version of Quaker faith and practice. I am delighted that they are also strong supporters of the historic and evolving Quaker testimonies on peace, equality, integrity, simplicity, civic engagement, and unity with nature.

Just last Saturday I co-led a workshop at Durham Friends Meeting, one of the few pastoral Quaker congregations in my area. Their pastor kindly asked me to stay over to worship with them on Sunday morning and to give the main message as a guest minister. We started the morning with silence while sitting in pews all facing the front of the room, sang hymns requested by people in the congregation, listened to a prepared Bible reading, sank back into silence, and then I stood and spoke for a quarter of an hour at the pulpit, giving the prepared sermon. We then entered into open silent worship again, during which different people spontaneously gave ministry from the congregation. It was a somewhat new and different form of Quaker worship for me, a variation on a theme, yet was as deep as the worship that I was used to.

If you would like, I could send you more information about these pastoral Quaker meetings. Personally, though, I am still much more powerfully drawn to "my" wing of the modern Quaker movement, in which there is no pastor, we sit facing each other, we gather and remain in deep silent worship for much longer periods of time, and it is much more common to include "non-Christian" Quakers, unorthodox followers of Jesus like myself, as well as more traditional "Christ-Centered" Quakers, all in one worshiping community.

To me, as long as we are seeking to follow in the way of Jesus and are open to the guidance of the Inward Teacher, regardless of what words or traditions most excite our minds, I feel we will have sufficient unity to be a vibrant, world-changing, spiritual community in the challenging times ahead. What do you think?

Affectionately,
Steve

LETTER 3

Silent Worship and the Inward Teacher

Dear Pat,

Thank you for your last letter. I am pleased that you resonate with the idea that a group of people can find deep spiritual unity and wisdom, even if they don't always hold identical beliefs about what you called "the big cosmological status of Jesus." This is done among "my" stream of the Quakers, just as you say, by turning toward the Inward Teacher together in silent waiting worship and opening ourselves to the direct experience of divine love and guidance as a group.

For me, silent Quaker worship is one of the loveliest wildflowers in the garden of the world's spiritual practices. It sounds like you are interested in learning more about it. I will try to answer your questions as best as I can. Yet, I encourage you to experiment with Quaker worship firsthand and attend some Quaker meetings for worship in your area. Direct experience is almost always preferable to words on a page—as helpful as words can be. If you are interested in doing this, you can find the Quaker meetings in your local area by going to the Quaker Finder website at www.quakerfinder.org.

Also, before I try to explain what I can about Quaker worship, I have to offer a big disclaimer here: "results may vary when using this product!" I'm only half kidding. For example, both the early Quaker theologian Robert Barclay and I had very deep spiritual experiences the very first time we visited a

Quaker meeting for worship. This is not true for everyone. Margery Post Abbot, for example, describes this situation in her book on the Quaker way.

> The silence of Quaker Meeting for Worship has always been a part of my life. In the 1950s and 60s, as a child I sat each Sunday in the large Meeting room in Philadelphia, watching the sun filter through the blinds, listening to the words offered in worship. . . . Between Sundays and the Friends' school I attended on weekdays, I learned much about the Bible and Quaker history as I absorbed the culture around me. . . . Still, I did not know how to listen to the guidance of the Inward Teacher. Such prompting seemed only for the saints, or for those gifted in a way I was not.

This missing mystical element of Quaker worship finally broke through for Margery in 1991 when, "without warning," she says she was "suddenly confronted with the reality of the Eternal Presence" during a meeting for worship. Up until then, she had defined her Quaker faith "in terms of action: what Friends call the testimonies of peace, simplicity, equality, community and integrity." For her, "Mysticism was an abstract concept." Yet, this very important element of Quaker worship became vivid and alive, and is now a transforming experience at the very center of her spiritual life. I love how she describes this breakthrough:

> As soon as someone rose to offer vocal ministry, something inside me cracked and the tears flowed. . . . In that hour, my life-long sense of worthlessness was consumed in all encompassing love as I sat, enfolded in God's arms.

Today, she says, "my faith calls me to encourage all people to wait and to attend on the still, small voice which transforms the heart." This is an experience of Quaker worship that is common among many Quakers. But every person's story is unique.

Some newcomers have to overcome some unconscious assumptions that get in the way of fully experiencing the spiritual breadth and depth of Quaker worship. A great story about this comes from contemporary British Quaker Jim Pym's experience of meeting for worship. As Jim tells his story, "I was born and brought up in the Roman Catholic Church, and it was thought by all concerned—including myself—that I was going to be a priest." However, Jim soon started asking challenging questions of his childhood faith and ultimately left the church in his twenties. At this point, he started looking for an alternative philosophy and soon found Buddhism and learned to meditate.

This was not the last stop on his spiritual journey, however. When his first Buddhist meditation group folded after a year or so, a friend suggested that Jim attend a local Quaker meeting for worship. As his friend put it, "They have an hour's meditation on Sunday mornings." Jim started attending his local Friends meeting and felt remarkably at home in the weekly meditative silence of Quaker worship.

The first several Quaker meetings for worship he attended were entirely silent, so Jim reports that it came as "quite a shock when someone first stood up and spoke in what I later learned was called 'ministry,' and which is one of the things that differentiates Quaker worship from Buddhist meditation." This was a jarring reminder that he was not in a Buddhist group anymore, even though so much of the experience was similar. Jim decided that if he was going to keep coming to meeting for worship he needed to learn more about Quakers. He took advantage of the meeting's learning opportunities, read books, and asked questions.

Jim was increasingly drawn to Quaker worship, and he began to see it as an astonishingly simple "practical mysticism for ordinary people." He writes, "a meeting for worship occurs when two or more people come together to sit in silence, and wait to experience the presence of God." And, he's right. It can happen any place and any time. Many informal or special meetings for worship are held at different times and places for healing, witness, personal support, family prayer, or to honor and celebrate community events like weddings, births, and deaths. Meetings for business and committee meetings are also conducted within a meeting for worship.

Like Jim, I agree that a Quaker meeting for worship is fundamentally a group spiritual practice, even when only two or three are gathered together. Yet, I have sometimes sat in silent, expectant waiting worship all by myself, sometimes during the most difficult moments of my life. I remember one night in particular a few years back when I had a horrible fight with my wife. It was late at night and Katy and I were angry, hurt, and bitter. We had yelled some hateful things at each other and were lying in bed next to each other in a sullen, stubborn silence. After what seemed like hours of hell, Katy got up and left the room, slamming the door behind her. She was carrying her pillow and blanket, so I figured she intended to sleep on the couch.

I lay in the dark, feeling helpless and still fuming and aching inside. Thoughts ran through me like, "She'd better come right back now and apologize, or else we're finished." And "I sure as hell am not going out to her. It's her fault, and it's her move if she wants to save this marriage. I am so sick of these fights." I was desperate and lost, and in complete despair. I needed a shot of salvation, big time.

Out of nowhere, I had a crazy thought. Why not quiet my angry "monkey mind" (a term Buddhists use for our busy, reactive thoughts), and center down in a one-person meeting for worship right there in a dark bedroom in the middle of the night. I was lost, but I knew enough to turn to the Inward Teacher for guidance. I then sat up without turning on the light, put my feet on the floor, got comfortable, quieted my breathing, calmed myself as best I could, and I began settling into silent worship. Into this silent, expectant waiting, I prayed, "Please, Dear Spirit, show me how to make a way out of no way."

As I sat alone in the silence, I felt a question emerge that seemed like an answer. Yet, it seemed so trite and clichéd that I pushed it away for as long as I could. Finally, though, I let the question in: "What would Jesus do?"

My first answer came some minutes later, and it was both challenging and calming. I remembered that Jesus was pretty down on men divorcing their wives. OK, step one: don't divorce Katy. It actually felt good to have at least one thing settled. I kept sitting in the silence, however, wondering if there was anything more for me to discover in the midst of this unusual meeting for worship.

After a while, just breathing in and out, I also remembered how Jesus once said that both the sunlight and the rain fall on the just and the unjust alike. I'd always thought that this bit of scripture means that God's love is unconditional no matter how far someone misses the mark. That gave me hope. I felt it was just possible that I could love Katy even though she was so completely wrong. Thank you, Jesus!

After an inner chuckle that felt really good following all my anguish, I was reminded that Jesus had also admonished his followers not to take the speck out of another's eye until they had taken the log out of their own eye. At that moment, I didn't like that recommendation at all. My breathing got faster and tighter and I tried to argue with Jesus there in the middle of my darkened bedroom. Yet, I continued sitting on the bed in silent worship, finally letting this troubling bit of scripture drop like a stone into the deep pool of silent worship. My breathing slowed down once again.

Somewhere inside I finally felt my guard drop and I admitted, "OK, I might have done a few things I shouldn't have as the fight got more heated between us, and maybe I missed some opportunities to do a few loving things I should have done before things got so ugly and out of control." At this point, another glimmer of hope dawned in me: if I'm part of the problem, then I might actually be able to change something in my behavior and help shift us away from our angry impasse, at least a little bit.

Still, I didn't have a clue about what to do. Then, I remembered that Jesus didn't just rely on what he read about the great prophets or sages in his sacred scriptures. Instead, Jesus went directly to the spiritual headwaters of our faith tradition. Jesus prayed to God. He would sit in the wilderness, or in a garden, or alone in a dark room in the middle of the night (just like me) and open his torn and tempted heart to the love and guidance of the Divine Spirit in which we live, move, and breathe. Jesus and I had the same Inward Teacher.

I resisted this idea for a while, but I soon centered even deeper into the prayerful silence of worship and handed it all over to Spirit. Crazily, after several minutes, I felt a wave of profound love and compassion come over me and then I got my answer: "Dude, just go out to the living room, sit beside her, and tell her you love her, that you want to live with her for the rest of your life, and that you are absolutely sure you both can figure out the problem in the morning. Then, tell her that you want to sleep with her tonight and you want to hold her in your arms." I sat quietly for a little while longer until I felt that my odd little one-person meeting for worship was over. Now was the time to take what I experienced in worship into the world— or at least into my living room.

Well, I did just what the voice told me to, and doing it the Inward Teacher's way worked a miracle. Katy and I cried together, we hugged, we told each other how much we loved each other, and we finally went back to bed and fell asleep in each other's arms, saying we would figure everything out in the morning. Jesus says that the Community of God can grow like a tiny mustard seed into a large bush to feed the birds and offer shade to the animals. Katy and I slept in the Community of God that night, under the moon shade of that mustard bush, and I will never forget it.

Please keep in mind, Pat, that different people often experience Quaker worship in different ways. As Margery Post Abbot explains:

> This opening of the soul to the Divine Comforter is at the heart of Friends' encounter with the Light, whether it be by sudden, mystical experience, by a steady sense of the Spirit beginning in childhood, or by a gradual growth into awareness of the gentle nudges on the soul often named as intuition.

I have experienced all three types of healing moments in meetings for worship. I have also experienced meetings for worship that have felt spiritually dry or flat to me. Yet, even in these dry times, I still find worship a calming and useful part of my week. I am mindful in those times that a deeper, more moving awareness of divine grace and challenge returns to me often enough in Quaker worship that my life is regularly enriched with Spirit and I am made more tender and whole. That is what my wife says anyway, and she should know.

There are many different ways to describe Quaker worship. A friend of mine once said that Quaker worship is a lovely combination of Zen meditation, ethical Jewish prophesy, and a prayer gathering in the name of Jesus. Even some of my atheist friends seem to enjoy going to meeting for worship from time to time. It nurtures mindfulness they say. For me, meetings for worship—at their best—are akin to what I imagine as the sublime moments experienced by a group of people sitting in a club and listening to the inspired live jazz improvisations of John Coltrane, Miles Davis, Charlie Mingus, or Thelonious Monk.

I remember my high school art teacher inviting me over to his house and playing John Coltrane's *Meditations* album for me on his record player. At first, it all sounded like a confusing wall of sound to me, just like the noisy internal chatter of random thoughts, judgments, and impressions in my "monkey mind." But then, suddenly, I was inside the sacred music, loving it, tearing up and laughing, and rocking back and forth. I got it. And, in that moment, I said to my teacher, "This is exactly the shift that happens to me in Quaker meeting."

This is not "exactly" what happens to everyone in Quaker meeting. In fact, I have never heard any other person describe meeting for worship as wild, improvisational jazz. Nonetheless, there is an improvisational element to Quaker worship, which builds on the many standard spiritual "melodies" that worshipers in Quaker meetings riff on week after week. I guess that is one reason why I like to visit other Quaker meetings for worship when I travel. I also like attending the week-long annual gatherings of New England Yearly Meeting or Friends General Conference. There I can worship out of doors with a small group of Quakers early each morning before breakfast and also worship with several hundred Quakers in a big conference room later on in the day. In such large group settings, the people who are moved to give vocal ministry stand up out of silence and wait until a microphone is brought to them so everyone can hear their message. This is very different from the much smaller scale and informality of our weekly meetings for worship in Putney, and even more distant from the tiny house meetings for worship I experienced as a young teenager in Galesburg. Yet, all these kinds of meeting for worship have become precious to me.

I have recognized, though, that Quaker worship is not for everyone. I still laugh when I remember my mom's best friend barreling out of the special meeting for worship for marriage held by the DeKalb Friends Meeting on the day of my wedding.

It was Sally's first and last Quaker meeting for worship. She marched up to me after the wedding, hugged me close, and said, "Steve, I love you, but don't ever make me sit through anything like that again. It drove me nuts!"

Yet, unlike Sally, most of the other participants did have a profound and moving experience that day, including many who were experiencing Quaker worship for the first time. I heard from many friends and family members that they delighted in sitting together silently in a circle, closing their eyes in meditation about the sacred relationship of marriage and about our particular union. They relished the simplicity when I and my spouse ultimately rose out of the worshipful silence and exchanged promises directly to each other without the aid of a minister, and without my wife being "given away" by someone else. They also loved how the silence returned and then several people, including a couple of young kids in our meeting, spoke out of the silence to share their own heartfelt and spontaneous vocal messages to the whole group. As happens frequently at Quaker weddings, several of these first timers felt moved to stand and speak at this special meeting for worship.

It is possible, maybe even likely, that the experience of Quaker worship would be meaningful and spiritually important to you. What do you think? Could this be a valuable spiritual practice for you? Are you interested in listening to improvisational, spiritual jazz?

Affectionately,
Steve

LETTER 4

Ministering One to Another

Dear Pat,

I was tickled to read your last letter about attending your first Quaker meeting for worship. Good for you for going straight to direct experience!

I don't know where your spiritual journey will ultimately take you, but I enjoyed your description of the feeling of sinking into the silence and I'm glad that you want to go back again. I personally think that it is wise to attend at least a few Quaker meetings before making a decision about whether the spiritual practice of Quaker worship speaks to you. Each meeting for worship is its own unique experience, just as each snowflake has its own unique shape, even if at first glance they all look alike.

In worship today at Putney Friends Meeting, my friend Noah stood up in the silence and read a set of queries from New England Yearly Meeting's book of *Faith and Practice*. These particular questions for us to consider focused on the quality of our preparation and participation in meetings for worship.

> Are your meetings for worship held in expectant waiting for divine guidance? Are you faithful and punctual in attendance? Do you come in a spirit of openness with heart and mind prepared for communion with God? Do both silent and vocal ministry arise as a response to the leading of the Holy Spirit?

Do all other activities of your meeting find their inspiration in worship, and do they, in turn, help to uphold the worshipping group?

Noah added that although these queries are framed as "yes" or "no" questions, they help us explore how close or far from the mark we are in our own preparation and participation in meeting for worship, as well as how we are doing together as a spiritual community. Things change and often deepen over time.

While reading your letter, I was particularly struck by how you described the vocal ministry in the meeting for worship you attended. Personally, I love that it is central to Quaker faith and practice that we all minister to one another in worship. Quakers often say that we didn't abolish the ministers—we abolished the laity.

I was thrilled to hear that you were moved by both the silence and by most of the spoken ministry at your first Quaker meeting. I was particularly touched when you described how one woman seemed to be speaking right to you, saying exactly what you needed to hear in that particular moment, to open your heart and help you move forward in your life with more integrity and vision. There have also been many such times for me when spoken ministry hits home with particular power, as if the Inward Teacher is communicating directly to me through the voice of someone else in the room. This sounds like what happened to you at your meeting and I'm glad. It is one of the special gifts that are possible during Quaker worship. We often hear things that seem meant just for us and couldn't be better timed.

Still, just as you discovered, not all vocal ministry seems to hit home every time. And, yes, I have also occasionally thought, "How is that message helpful?" On those occasions, when a message doesn't speak to me, I try to trust that the message will be of value to someone else in the room. Sometimes I hold both the speaker and the other hearers in my heart and pray for the message to serve them well.

Something mysterious sometimes happens when people are drawn to give vocal ministry in a meeting for worship. For well over a year of attending Quaker worship, I never offered any vocal ministry. Yet, after several times of feeling a call to say something and suppressing it, I finally gave in, took the risk to stand up, and shared what I felt given to say. I don't remember if I offered a quote I had read somewhere, told a Bible story, or spoke about an insight or personal story. Yet, when I sat down, I felt I had been faithful in that moment and that I had played my part in our ministering one to another. I also felt scared and shaken. Who was I to stand up and give ministry at the age of fifteen?

At the end of the worship period, an older member of the meeting came over to me and said that the message I gave had touched and healed a tender, wounded place in her. I was astonished. What if I had suppressed the urge to stand and give vocal ministry that day? What if I had not been faithful to the inner prompting I experienced tugging at me?

In meetings for worship after that, I still sometimes found myself trying to suppress the inward nudge to stand and offer spoken ministry. Yet, whenever I felt too scared to speak, I asked myself, "Who might I be letting down if I don't stand and speak what has been given to me to say?" I started to think I might be suppressing something that is emerging from deep within the soul of the meeting that some folks needed to hear that day. Time and time again, reminding myself of this has helped me act faithfully when I am called to speak and reluctant to do it. It seems worth the risk of saying something embarrassing or sounding really stupid if the act of giving ministry might actually be of real use to somebody sitting in the circle.

In my late teens, however, I got much too free and easy with how often I stood to offer vocal ministry about almost anything that crossed my mind. I might have even been like the guy who stood up in your meeting and gave a message that felt kind of flat or off to you. Looking back, I was clearly getting too talkative and too full of myself as a minister. Quakers often call this "outrunning our Guide."

Sensing my problem, a woman on the meeting's ministry and counsel committee, which works to deepen our spiritual life together, encouraged me to ask myself three silent questions before speaking in worship. The first question was, is this a message of clear spiritual value, and is it really tugging at me? The second question was, is this message meant to be given to others or is it meant just for me? Finally, she encouraged me to ask a third question, one that I didn't completely understand at first: is it necessary that I stand and give this message, or might someone else offer the same message today?

This last question only fully made sense to me much later, after I had a surprising experience in meetng for worship. On that particular day, I felt a strong sense of being called to offer a message in worship. It didn't feel like just my ego talking or my wanting to show off. It felt true, deep, and valuable, and it also felt like a message that was not just for me, but for many in the room. The impulse wouldn't go away. In fact, it got stronger in intensity as time passed. I hesitated just a bit longer while contemplating the third question about whether I was the one to offer this ministry. To my surprise, within just a few moments, someone else stood up and offered a message so close to what I had felt called to share that I was stunned.

That day I learned to trust that if a message is really meaningful and knocking on my door, it might also be knocking on someone else's door. This was a humbling and delightful discovery. I discovered once again just how much of a mystery shared worship in Quaker meeting can be.

In my wing of the Quaker movement, most of the vocal ministry offered in worship emerges spontaneously, unplanned, and in the moment. Yet, there are occasions for prepared ministry as well. For example, when Noah read the queries this morning, that was an act of planned ministry. Every third Sunday of the month, someone from the ministry and counsel committee reads a different set of queries. This is a fairly new practice for us. Only a few months ago we decided that this exercise might deepen our worship and spiritual community. Already it has meant a lot to me, and I think to others.

Another example of prepared ministry occurs at the summer sessions of New England Yearly Meeting. Several months in advance, a planning committee identifies a person to present a message to gathering participants on the topic chosen for that year. In 2011, the theme was how might a broken people help heal a broken planet, a concern close to my own heart. I was tapped to offer prepared ministry on Sunday afternoon at the gathering. My charge was to rise out the silence of worship and give a message to over 450 Quakers for 45 to 50 minutes, while speaking into a microphone at a podium. I was both frightened and excited to rise to this challenge.

Blessedly, my spiritual community *ministered to me* as I prepared to minister to others. For example, I was encouraged to follow a Quaker tradition of asking a spiritual companion to accompany me in my preparations. I asked my friend Noah to serve in that role and he generously agreed. This formal relationship with Noah was a huge help to me. He would often call or write me in the months I was preparing my vocal ministry for yearly meeting. He listened to my hopes and dreams, noticed my stuck places, reminded me to be patient, and even agreed to introduce me with a song that had touched me deeply when he sang it in meeting for worship some months earlier.

I was also "held in the Light" that day by Noah and close to twenty other members of Putney Friends Meeting who traveled to Rhode Island and sat on the "facing bench" behind the podium as I spoke. I almost broke down crying as I thanked them at the beginning of my talk for ministering to me by sitting with me, holding me in the Light, and lending their presence to support the message I had come to share with our yearly meeting. As Noah said in his introduction, "It takes a meeting to raise a ministry."

My meeting ministered to me in another important way. Months before the talk, they offered to set up an ongoing ministry oversight committee for me. I accepted and they found four members of our meeting to serve in this capacity. These gifted people encouraged me, made me laugh, raised loving challenges, listened to me deeply, and expressed their responses to my work. They helped me stay centered, worshipful, accountable to Putney Friends Meeting, and "in the Life and the Power." My plenary talk was well received in no small measure because of the work of these four people from my meeting.

Today, this committee continues to meet with me about once a month as I am increasingly being invited to speak at other Quaker gatherings, to give guest sermons for other religious communities, and to give talks on faith-based activism. If there was ever any doubt in my mind, this experience has made it abundantly clear that vocal ministry is only just one of the ways we "minister one to another" in a Quaker meeting. Let me share some other examples that are represented by just four individuals I was talking with before meeting for worship last week.

One of these folks rarely offers vocal ministry in our meetings for worship. Yet, he rides his bike—rain, snow, or shine—to the meeting house every Sunday morning before anyone else arrives. If the heater needs to be on, he turns it on. If the sidewalk and stairs need to be shoveled, he shovels them. He frequently stands at the door as people arrive and welcomes them. If he spots newcomers, he spends a little more time welcoming them, letting them know where to hang their coats, where the meeting room and bathrooms are, and answering any questions they may have. This is his ministry.

The second person I was talking to has given powerful vocal ministry in meetings for worship, but again only rarely. She mainly ministers to our spiritual community by serving as the clerk of our meeting. She tracks details, manages the meeting's correspondence, makes sure all our committees are functioning well, and offers support, encouragement, and loving challenge when needed. She reads beautiful, carefully selected quotations to signal the shift from silence to thoughtful discussion at our monthly meetings for business. She is also a loving and skillful facilitator at these meetings, keeping us grounded as we seek together for God's will, and then, without any vote being taken, she has a knack for finding and reflecting back the "sense of the meeting" as she listens to both our silences and our talk. This is her ministry.

The third person has served for many years on our ministry and counsel committee. He is attentive and skillful at noticing the spiritual condition of individuals in our meeting and of the group as a whole. He greets people warmly at potlucks even though he is shy. He listens to them, visits members at home sometimes, or invites them to his home for a meal. He has arranged for practical help and moral support when people in our meeting are having a tough time. At the close of our regular meetings for worship, he often stands and asks if anyone has any "after thoughts," or joys or concerns that they would like to share with the whole group before we move on to announcements. This is his ministry.

The last person I was talking to has played several important community roles in her many years as a member of our meeting. She is perhaps best known as a champion of the Quaker testimony on equality and inclusiveness, and she has often been active on our social justice and peace committee, as well as the ministry and council committee. More recently, she has served as a sounding board and voice of encouragement for neighbors who have been active in starting up the wildly successful Transition Putney initiative to help Putney village move from oil dependence to local resilience. In our business meetings, she is tough, almost brutally honest, and has a great laugh. She is also remarkably patient and loving, something she tells me she had to learn over time. She can now sit in the fire of controversy and model calm, compassionate listening and prophetic witness at the same time. This is her ministry.

Stories like these can be told about almost any member or regular attender at Putney Friends Meeting. Some people have come to meeting for years, have never given vocal ministry in meeting for worship, but have brought soup to potlucks or mopped the floor week after week. Hopefully, this letter has given you a better sense of what Quakers mean when we say that we are all involved in ministering one to another. As noted in New England Yearly Meeting's book of *Faith and Practice*:

> The membership of a Friends Meeting, or of the Society of Friends, is made up of persons with varying gifts or abilities. Each gift or each type of ability may be a form of ministry, and hence leadership. . . . Some members have gifts of teaching and counseling, or of organization and administration, or of vocal ministry or public speaking, or other similar gifts which identify them as leaders. Members with other gifts are not simply passive followers, but all are co-workers in the care and nurture of the body and its members. And all are co-workers in witness to our faith and in the service of love and justice among people and nations.

Shared vocal ministry, and our time together in meeting for worship, are only one part of what makes us a vibrant spiritual community. We all have spiritual gifts to share, and all these gifts are needed. At our best, we help identify and nurture these gifts and abilities in each other.

If you keep attending meeting for worship and get more involved in the Quaker community close to you, be on the lookout for all these forms of shared ministry. What might your spiritual gifts be? Does anything already come to mind?

Affectionately,
Steve

LETTER 5

Quaker Faith and Social Action

Hi Pat,

I really enjoyed your last letter. I'm glad you've gone back to your local Quaker meeting for worship a few more times and that you are still finding it meaningful to you. And I laughed when you reported chatting with various folks about the Quaker movement and how you are now able to fill in a lot of blanks in people's understanding of the Quaker way.

I was touched, too, that when your friend was joking about Quakers being "knee-jerk liberal do-gooders," you took the time to explain that Quaker activism is not beholden to any political party and is much more than some secular ideological preference. Many people do have a "do-gooder" image of us because so many Quakers choose to work in the helping professions, to engage with socially responsible businesses, and to take part in nonviolent social movements for peace, justice, and sustainability. And yet, you were right in explaining that this is an outward expression of an inward spiritual experience, an expression of values that emerge from our worship as well as the longstanding prophetic calling of our spiritual community. Here's how it is expressed in one of the "Advices" from my yearly meeting's book of *Faith and Practice*:

Friends are called, as followers of Christ, to help establish the Kingdom of God on earth. Let us strengthen a sense of kinship with everyone. Let that sense of kinship inspire us in our efforts to build a social order free of violence and oppression, in which no person's development is thwarted by poverty and the lack of health care, education, or freedom. Friends are advised to minister to those in need, but also to seek to know the facts and the causes of social and economic ills and to work for the removal of those ills. Let us cherish every human being and encourage efforts to overcome all forms of prejudice.

This spiritual work of taking social action in the wider world has been evident in our faith and practice, in a variety of forms, from the beginning. Quaker entrepeneurs have been widely respected for fair and honest business dealings, for starting innovative enterprises to benefit workers and the community, and for efforts to avoid trading in products produced by slave labor or other socially harmful means, as well as to avoid investments in the machinery of war. Quakers have been involved in developing various social services, including reforms of prisons and mental health care and programs for support of refugees, to name just a few. And even in the face of persecution and repression, many Quakers have engaged in nonviolent direct action and civil disobedience to support the Underground Railroad, abolition, women's suffrage, economic justice, civil rights, peace, and earthcare.

As a community of spiritual seekers, Quakers have also sought to encourage each other to learn the core values of simplicity, integrity, nonviolence, equality, ecological stewardship, and community service that undergird our daily practices and social witness in the world. Now, it is true that even our best spiritual teachers only echo and amplify the motions of the Holy Spirit in our hearts. Yet, the spiritual teaching we offer each other is precious and needed to encourage our most faithful efforts to heal and mend the wounded world around us. Without such teachers and such teachings, it would be so much easier to ignore the Spirit and miss the mark dramatically.

In this light, my mother was my first spiritual teacher. I still remember how, when I was a little boy, my mom would call me into the family room to watch the TV news with her whenever a story about the civil rights movement came on. In this way, snuggled up against her and with her arm around me, I became aware of the freedom rides, the Southern Christian Leadership Conference, the Student Nonviolent Coordinating Committee, Martin Luther King, and the March on Washington. I particularly remember watching the footage of the demonstrations in Birmingham, Alabama. This was when Bull Conner ordered the fire houses turned on black men, women, and children who were merely marching for their rights. I saw the water blasting from the fire hoses and slamming these people against walls and knocking them to the ground. I was horrified, but I was also awed and inspired as these people kept standing up again. My mom said to me as we watched, "Stevie, these are God's people. I want you to be like them when you grow up."

Not surprisingly, Martin Luther King became my second spiritual teacher. At the time, I saw King as an almost larger than life example of soulful faithfulness, resolute moral leadership, nonviolent courage in the face of violence and hatred, and an enduring commitment to creating "the Beloved Community," his modern term for what Jesus and the prophets had called the "Kingdom of God." I am certainly not the only Quaker who has been profoundly inspired by King's deep integration of religious faith and nonviolent social action. Indeed, King was invited to give the 1958 keynote address at the annual Friends General Conference Gathering. There he explained to the assembled Quakers from all over the country the lessons he had gleaned from the Montgomery bus boycott on the importance of nonviolent social action as key part of following Jesus faithfully. It wasn't until many years later that I actually heard the recording of that talk, but I had already read numerous books both by and about King, found in the libraries of every Quaker meeting in which I have been active. Bayard Rustin, a Quaker activist, was among King's closest advisors and the lead organizer for the famous 1963 March on Washington.

I think King's idea of "creative maladjustment" is a very helpful concept in understanding the Quaker commitment to our social testimonies and so often engaging in many kinds of social action to help build up the Kingdom of God in our personal lives, our spiritual communities, our workplaces, our communities, and the wider world. In his book *Strength to Love*, which I first found in the library of my meeting when I was a teenager, King helped me better understand the broad social mission of my Quaker faith. As he put it:

> This hour in history needs a dedicated circle of transformed nonconformists. Our planet teeters on the brink of annihilation; dangerous passions of pride, hatred, and selfishness are enthroned in our lives; and men do reverence before false gods of nationalism and materialism. The saving of our world from pending doom will come, not through the complacent adjustment of the conforming majority, but through the creative maladjustment of a nonconforming minority.

For King, being well-adjusted to a world marred by oppression, violence, and indifference was not only pathological, but also unfaithful. In this book, King tried to impart the same deep spiritual wisdom that the apostle Paul expressed to the new followers of the Jesus movement who lived in the capital city of the Roman Empire. As Paul advised this new spiritual community that lived in the very belly of the beast, "Do not conform to this world, but be transformed by the renewing of your minds, so that you may discern what is the will of God— what is good and acceptable and perfect."

Similarly, many Quakers throughout our history have lived lives of radical nonconformity to the unjust and militaristic customs of the society in which they find themselves. They view such nonconformity as a core feature of our spiritual vocation as a faithful people of God. Many of us have come to believe that anything less than creative maladjustment to an oppressive world is not faithful, but the learned helplessness of denial, distraction, or despair that causes us to get too comfortable with conformity and complicity.

It should not come as any surprise, then, that my third spiritual teacher was the Quaker community itself. As a young teenage Quaker in the late 1960s and early 1970s, I loved reading the many stories of creative maladjustment that came from the early days of the Quaker movement. For example, early Quakers were frequently ridiculed and ostracized for their refusal to obey the deeply ingrained social customs that protected the hierarchical privileges of social class. They would not bow or take their hats off for the rich and the noble. They would not call anyone, even royalty, by flattering titles or use fancy figures of speech in addressing them. They refused to wear fashionable clothing or swords, and instead wore simple garments and avoided all forms of conspicuous consumption. As Robert Barclay explained it back in 1692, whenever we "are not content to make proper use of the creation, trouble begins."

Many early Quakers were also unpopular among leading sectors of their communities for campaigning against the slave trade, championing responsible business practices, refusing to join the King's army, and pushing for religious liberty. In the early years of the movement, Quakers were frequently thrown in prison for refusing to pay tithes to the state church, for refusing to swear oaths in British courts, for worshiping openly, and for speaking of their faith at public meetings and in pamphlets and broadsides. Many were imprisoned for blasphemy, and some were even tortured or hanged.

Understandably, as the authors of many early Quaker journals attest, the spiritual calling to defy social conventions and act on their values often sparked an inner and sometimes painful struggle with temptation and fear. Comfortable conformity and moral complacency is a much easier path than personal and social action. These early Quakers had to face some of their deepest anxieties, become willing to appear foolish in the eyes of others, and learn to take public action in alignment with their deepest faith commitments. This was not easy, but these Quakers listened carefully to the still, small voice of the Spirit in worship and prayer, and they were frequently inspired by the example, and sometimes by the gentle challenge, of others in their spiritual community.

As a Quaker teenager, I completely resonated with how these early Quakers found prophetic social action to be a natural outgrowth of the inner spiritual experience. This sense of prophetic spiritual calling is also still true for many Quakers today. I mean "prophetic" here not in the sense of predicting the future, but in the sense of a people answering the spiritual call to seek justice, practice compassion, and walk humbly with our God in every aspect of our lives. As you noted to your friends, many Quakers today are involved in some aspect of healing our wounded world through our vocations, our community volunteering, our political engagement, and our work to remove the seeds of war, exploitation, or ecological unraveling from our households and our personal lives.

One of my favorite examples of bold social action in the world today is the Earth Quaker Action Team (EQAT), a group of Quaker activists from different local meetings in Pennsylvania, New Jersey, Delaware, and the District of Columbia. The team's members are like many Quakers and others who, because of their faith, recycle and re-use, drive hybrids and bicycles, and take buses and shorter showers whenever they can. Yet EQAT has also concluded "that the sum of individual actions cannot make up for the destructive decisions taken by large structures." They have come to believe that they also need to confront what the Bible calls "the powers and principalities" that undergird the structures of environmental destruction and social oppression.

Currently EQAT is focusing its attention on PNC Bank. Once a small Quaker-owned bank, PNC is now the fifth-largest bank in the United States in terms of deposits. PNC has described itself as "America's greenest bank," although it is the number one financer of mountaintop removal, a method of mining coal that destroys forests and wildlife and is extremely harmful to the water supply and public health.

Initially, EQAT members sought dialogue with local branch managers and upper management of the bank. When these efforts at communication did not meet with a positive response, they marched in solidarity with community activists in West Virginia calling for an end to mountaintop removal mining, occupied several local bank branches in the region with other faith-based activists, and then in 2011 conducted a highly visible nonviolent civil disobedience action at the PNC booth at the Philadelphia Flower Show (of which PNC was a sponsor).

The Earth Quaker Action Team has also been calling on Quakers, and other people of good will, to join them in a "move your money" campaign, asking depositors to withdraw their money from PNC and put it into more responsible local banks and credit unions until PNC changes its policies. This strategy allows participants to use their financial resources with greater moral integrity and purpose, a practice that has been spiritually important for Quakers from the very beginning. Just this week, I learned that Philadelphia Yearly Meeting, which holds a number of funds, has decided to close all their current accounts with PNC and move their money to more socially responsible financial institutions.

All this effort was followed by the bank making a public statement that in the future they intend not to invest in or lend money to companies that make a majority of their profits from mountaintop removal coal mining. The social action campaign continues, though, to strengthen the terms of this initial pledge and to make sure this policy is actually implemented. This is just one powerful example of the relationship between Quaker faith and social action.

I have recently made the personal journey from supporting the nonviolent civil disobedience actions of others to actually engaging in such witness myself. Last March, I got arrested for marching with 130 other people onto the property of the Louisiana-based Entergy Corporation's Brattleboro, Vermont, headquarters. We had gone to their offices to deliver a message insisting they shut down the Vermont Yankee nuclear reactor, an old, accident-prone facility, which is now operating in violation of Vermont state law.

My journey to committing civil disobedience was not merely a personal choice, however. It emerged out of a collective effort among Quakers in our region to discern a faithful response to the likely possibility that the Entergy Corporation would refuse to close the reactor as promised if it did not receive a new "certificate of public good" from the state after its operating license expired in March of 2012. The Burlington Friends Meeting engaged in deep silent prayer, thoughtful reflection, and substantive discussions of this issue over a series of monthly business meetings. In May 2011, they finally came to unity on the issue and approved a minute (a written decision) that said, in part:

> To say "No" to nuclear fission here in Vermont is to say "Yes" to being a different people: to overcome our fear of powerlessness and become hopeful and courageous. It is to become radically more simple in our patterns of living, consuming far less energy and material things. If we choose to be a different people it will become much clearer what we, as Friends, must do.

Among the many faithful actions endorsed by Burlington Friends Meeting was their encouragement for Burlington Quakers to "join with those called to public witness, including non-violent civil disobedience, to shut down our own nuclear power plant, Vermont Yankee, and continue to speak to public officials on this matter."

Burlington Friends sent copies of their minute to Vermont legislators and all the Quaker meetings in Vermont, New Hampshire, and Massachusetts whose members and attenders would be directly affected by an accident at the aging reactor. They urged other Quakers in the region either to adopt their minute, or to create their own minutes on this pressing concern.

At Putney Friends Meeting, we began our consideration of this issue in worshipful silence. As is our practice, we then moved into thoughtful discussion, often punctuated by periods of silent reflection between spoken messages. This discussion was facilitated by our clerk and grounded in an attempt to discern a faithful way forward for the all the members and attenders of our meeting. We listened carefully to each other and tried not to interrupt each other, even when we initially disagreed with something that someone said.

As in all Quaker business meetings, our goal was to develop a heartfelt sense of spiritual unity on this issue—a unity that was not based on any kind of majority vote or lowest common denominator compromise, but was faithful to our very best collective understanding of divine will on this matter. Finding such unity required us as individuals to listen carefully, and to resist the temptation to try to swing others to our own points of view. While we did not all start out in complete agreement with each other, or with the minute from the Quakers in Burlington, a spiritual consensus did begin to emerge. We then asked two members of our meeting to reflect together on what they had heard in our discussions and prepare a draft minute for members to consider at our next meeting for business. This proposed minute was considered a month later and approved by all in attendance, with only a few minor changes.

Putney Friends declared, "As members of the Religious Society of Friends, we believe we are called to be good stewards of the earth." Our minute also said, in part:

> We are made to be an integral part of this wondrous Creation. Let us choose now to take up our stewardship commitment, fully accepting our responsibilities to care for our planet and its peoples. Let us choose now to join with other Friends, and all people of good will and understanding, to move forward through worship and through witness to accomplish our goals.

And after detailing our concerns about the reactor, we stated in even more specific terms:

> Putney Friends Meeting firmly supports the Vermont state government's efforts to close the Vermont Yankee nuclear power plant by March 21, 2012. We call on all our members and attenders to consider joining the citizen's movement working to enforce the people's will on this matter, up to and including nonviolent protest and civil disobedience.

These were not empty words on paper either. Our social justice and peace committee began preparations that included a presentation for the meeting. Some members got training in nonviolent action, in preparation for getting arrested or for a support role to others. And we took part in other activities building up to March 22, 2012, the day following expiration of the reactor's license. On that day, approximately one thousand people rallied to hear supportive messages from the governor of Vermont and about twenty Vermont state representatives and senators. One representative is a member of our meeting and his primary Quaker witness is to serve in the state legislature with integrity, compassion, and civic concern. Everyone then marched to the Entergy headquarters where several Quakers from my meeting and others were among the 130 arrested that day for committing civil disobedience.

As glad as I am to have finally gotten over my own fear of

being arrested, most of my faith-based social action involves how I choose to live my life, what kind of work I do for a living, and the many other forms of civic engagement and volunteering in the community that I regularly engage in. All of these are faithful outward expressions of my inward experience of Quaker worship and my encounter with the Inward Teacher.

There is no one right way of engaging in faithful social action. Nor does it normally require dramatic public action. In fact, one of the activities that brought me the most joy in recent months was helping with the public launch of the Friendly Households Challenge, a project of the Eco-Justice Working Group of Philadelphia Yearly Meeting. This is a cooperative project to help Quakers in local meetings provide mutual aid, education, and support to each other as they look for more effective ways to follow the Quaker testimonies of integrity, simplicity, the fair sharing of the world's resources, and ecological stewardship. Their vision is for Quakers everywhere to become part "of a Great Turning toward peace, justice, ecological balance, and more durable, local economies" through how we live our personal and household lives.

In my presentation at the launch of this project, I told the participants a story I first heard a couple of decades ago. Back in the 1980s, a coalition of churches, civic groups, and small business leaders organized a campaign in Seattle to honor Martin Luther King. They eventually got the city council to agree to change the name of the main street running through Seattle's predominantly black neighborhood to "Martin Luther King, Jr. Way." At the victory celebration, Vincent Harding, a longtime associate of King, spoke to the community. Harding urged everyone there to fully embrace the deep symbolism of what they had just accomplished. First, he reminded people that the road used to be named the "Empire Way." Then, he said, "Think of it! You have now changed the road you travel from the Empire Way to Martin's Way."

Isn't that one of our core spiritual challenges today, changing the road we travel from the empire way to King's vision of the "Beloved Community?" Isn't this what the prophets, Jesus, and the Inward Teacher all call out to us to do? Isn't this a core part of what being faithful means? Well, it is certainly what my mother called on me to do, and I still agree with her spiritual teaching. It is also what Quakers, at our best, have repeatedly been called to do for over 350 years.

So, here are my questions for you: How do you see the role of social action in your spiritual life? Do you see it as deeply rooted in your own faith and inward spiritual experience? Do you think it would help you to be part of spiritual community that seeks to encourage diverse forms of faithfulness in its members? I can't wait to hear more about your thoughts on this.

Affectionately,
Steve

LETTER 6
The Struggle To Be Faithful

Dear Pat,

I was moved to read in your last letter about how you are coming to feel a growing affinity with the spiritual path of Quakers. As you say, the Quaker way combines an inward mystical communion with the Spirit, an intimate engagement with an ongoing spiritual community, and the practice of peaceful social witness and active healing in the wider world through our families, our vocations, our consumption, and our civic activity. The way you describe all this is beautiful, and I think that you have gotten right to the heart of the matter. Thanks for sharing your thoughts with me on all this.

I was also pleased to read that you are becoming a bit more than an occasional attender at your Quaker meeting. They are lucky to have you and I hope that you continue to find rest, challenge, delight, wisdom, guidance, and community through your participation with the meeting near you. I wish you well on this journey of spiritual discovery, wherever it takes you.

One thing I want to address in this letter, though, is your worry that you might not be "radical enough or faithful enough to be a Quaker." I hope I haven't created an unrealistic image of the Quaker movement that makes it sound as if Quakers are paragons of the faithful life, or that all Quakers are involved in dramatic social change efforts. We are not. We all have personal failings, treat our loved ones and fellow meeting members poorly at times, and are sometimes so caught up in denial or despair that we don't seize the opportunity to stand up for our principles in our various spheres of influence. In fact, back in my mid-20s, I started judging the Religious Society of Friends pretty harshly for not being good enough, radical enough, or faithful enough.

I am not proud of it, but I drifted away from Quakers for several years because of my own youthful disappointment with the Quaker movement. First, I was disillusioned by what I saw as my meeting's lack of pastoral care and integrity when one of our families was in real trouble. Second, I increasingly felt that most modern Quakers had grown too comfortable, lacked prophetic fire, and were far too content just to hold their beliefs privately and not act on them in the wider world in any meaningful way. I yearned for Quakers to work more with our neighbors to make real and tangible improvements in the balance of power and the ethical tone in our society. I felt that Quakers had drifted too far away from following in the footsteps of Jesus and his liberating gospel. It seemed to me that the modern Quaker movement had become much too "conformed to this world."

During my "interlude" away from the Quaker movement, I still cherished my teenage and early adult years as a Quaker and all that they had given me. I made some sporadic efforts to attend meeting in other locations as I moved around the country, but I never felt as spiritually at home as I yearned to feel and I soon dropped away each time. Still, the memory and power of meeting for worship tugged at me. I missed my Quaker spiritual practice and my active association with the Religious Society of Friends. But for the longest time, I never seemed to find a strong enough inner leading to go back and fully re-engage.

This spiritual stuckness finally began to shift for me, slowly and incrementally. I became increasingly conscious that I had generalized too much from my experiences with one meeting, at one particular time, and had unjustly projected this specific experience onto the whole of the Religious Society of Friends. More importantly, I began to feel real compassion and forgiveness for the specific Quakers that I had felt let down by. We all have blind spots and failings. I now know that I have more than my fair share, both large and small.

You may laugh, or even be angry with me, but just last week I violated one of my principles and gave into temptation by eating at Burger King. I did this even though I support buying from local businesses instead of large corporate chains, and even though I know that fast food meat is raised unsustainably and often involves animal cruelty and exploitative labor practices. I had lots of local, affordable and healthy alternatives to choose from, and I wasn't even in a hurry that day. The moral hypocrisy of all this did not escape me when I parked my car in the Burger King lot, with my three bumper stickers on the back saying, "We Support Local Farmers," "No Farms, No Food," and "Think Locally, Act Locally."

I was out of integrity in that moment, but unable to resist. Ever since my childhood, when my mother was a hardworking single mom with little energy left over at the end of day to cook meals, I have felt that a meal made up of a Whopper, fries, and a Coke was a real treat. My mother and I ate at Burger King two or three times a week for years because it was quick, convenient, and cheap, but this addictive, "comfort food" habit from childhood still exercises a powerful hold on me. Of course, my missing the mark last week does not mean that I am no longer qualified to be a member of a Quaker meeting. As the elderly woman in Galesburg told me back in 1968, "You will always be welcome at a Quaker meeting." This is just as true for you and any other sincere spiritual seeker.

The Quaker way is about engaging in a spiritual journey, about moving toward greater wholeness and integrity over time with the help of both the Spirit and our spiritual community. It is not about judging ourselves, or each other in our very real struggles to be faithful. It is not even about having the same idea of what choices are "faithful." This, anyway, is the understanding that I finally came to, after too many years away. I eventually felt led to come back home to my spiritual community with a new patience, a new humility, and a new maturity. This slow spiritual reawakening ultimately led me to the Putney Friends Meeting, where we are increasingly loving to each other and growing in both spiritual wisdom and prophetic fire as time goes on.

Can we really expect more from each other than this? There is a story in the gospel of Matthew demonstrating that even Jesus was not always "perfect" and had to grow into greater wholeness, integrity, and compassion as he matured. In my Bible, the story is entitled "The Canaanite Woman's Faith." Jesus and several of his disciples are just returning to their lodgings after a long day of healing and preaching when a Canaanite woman runs after them. She shouts, "Have mercy on me, Lord," and asks him to heal her desperately ill daughter. It is a heart-wrenching moment.

But, here is where the story gets even more heartbreaking. Jesus and the disciples hear her desperate cries and choose to ignore her and her appeal for help. Without addressing her, they ridicule her among themselves. They want her to go away and leave them alone. Why? It appears that they were prejudiced against her because she was not part of their ethnic group, not sufficiently part of their circle of moral concern. As Jesus says to his disciples, "I was sent only to the lost sheep of the house of Israel."

When the Canaanite woman finally catches up to them, the disciples try to send her away. Yet she will not be put off. Her concern for her daughter and her faith in Jesus as a healer are just too intense. She throws herself at his feet and shouts up at him, "Lord, help me." Instead of responding with kindness, Jesus now insults her directly to her face. He says, "It is not fair to take the children's food and throw it to the dogs." But, again, this woman will not be put off by this attempt to shame and repel her. With both humor and fierce intelligence she tries one more time to melt Jesus's hardened heart, saying, "Yes, Lord, but even the dogs eat the crumbs that fall from their master's table."

At this point in the story, a small miracle happens. Jesus suddenly sees this woman as a person fully worthy of his moral consideration and concern. He is filled with compassion for her and expands his very notion of what loving your neighbor really means. He is converted to a deeper, more profound love and no longer conforms to the narrow prejudices of his upbringing. Jesus lifts the woman to her feet and says, "Woman, great is your faith." The story ends with the words, "And her daughter was healed instantly."

We follow Jesus best then by seizing the opportunities to participate in a faithful spiritual transformation of our limited beliefs, behaviors, and compulsions as we become more obedient to the Spirit. Quakers, at our best, have repeatedly gone through this often difficult, but beautiful process of moving beyond the various ways our hearts are hardened and conformed to this world, and entering into a deeper understanding of the Beloved Community and what real faithfulness requires of us. Quakers have an impressive history of this kind of transformation, and there are also many times when we have missed the mark for years and years, even decades.

When I first became a Quaker, I was often told proud stories about how Quakers were the first religious denomination in America to formally declare slavery to be wrong and to banish the practice among all their members. These colonial Friends were certainly ahead of their time, as this was accomplished before the American Revolution. Personally, though, I was a little shocked that even a small percentage of Quakers had ever owned slaves given our belief in there being "that of God" in everyone. Yet I could understand the powerful pull that being part of a dominant culture can exert on one's moral imagination. My own memory was still fresh about how, as a young kid, I had been an ardent supporter of the U.S. war against Vietnam. I therefore felt both humbled and proud that early Quakers in America had made the shift from the sin of slavery to the faithfulness of emancipation.

What I didn't fully realize back then is how difficult this turn toward faithfulness was to accomplish. As I learned later, it took colonial Quakers close to a hundred years to discern together what seems so obvious to us now, that the institution of slavery should be abandoned and the emancipation of all God's children should be supported. As noted in the remarkable Quaker history book *Fit For Freedom, Not For Friendship*:

> Friends in the 1700s were likely to view enslavement from one of four perspectives. A majority of Quakers accepted slavery "without much qualm or question." Others were "perplexed, but did nothing." Still others agreed with George Fox ... that slaves should be treated "kindly" and offered a Christian education—a line of thought that did not embrace emancipation. Finally, a "sensitive few" doubted if Christians should be enslaving their fellow men.

These "sensitive few" labored with their Quaker sisters and brothers for close to a hundred years to finally turn the whole Society to a new standard of faithfulness. It is also humbling to know that even after all the decades it took for all Quakers to embrace the firm conviction that slavery was wrong and that emancipating their slaves was God's will, only a minority of Quakers went on to join with their neighbors to build up a broad-based abolition movement. Indeed, some Quaker activists who joined with secular abolition organizations were admonished or dismissed from their meetings as being "too worldly." Many Quaker schools also remained segregated up until the mid-twentieth century. Dealing with the legacy of racism in our midst is still a struggle and a learning journey among Quakers today.

Patricia Loring says in her pamphlet *Spiritual Discernment* that the Quaker movement has long "held the expectation that God would raise up prophets within the community to speak to people for the good of the community and the world." In my own spiritual journey, I try to live faithfully, and I also cultivate compassion for both myself and others who are caught in this sometimes painful, but liberating process of spiritual growth and redemption. I live right now in the middle of this paradox of urgency and patience. Does this paradox seem familiar to you?

My own meeting has made such a painful but rewarding transition to greater faithfulness in its decision to support full marriage equality for all people, gay and straight. Most of this shift was made before I started attending Putney Friends Meeting, but I love hearing the stories about this time from folks who have been around longer.

These issues were first openly discussed at the meeting in the 1970s. Wide differences of opinion were expressed and were often a source of anger, frustration, and conflict in our meeting. When I talk to some of the older gay and lesbian members who were engaged in these discussions, I am impressed with their steadfastness. They were often hurt by the remarks of people who opposed gay and lesbian rights, including marriage equality, and who often made harsh statements about gay and lesbian people.

Yet, these gay and lesbian members and attenders hung in there. They did not back down, did not leave in a huff, but actively persevered, year after year, in search of a path to mutually respectful dialogue that would help the meeting identify a good and faithful way forward. Several people among those who initially disagreed with our "sensitive few," also promoted greater compassion and respectful dialogue, even as they still had fears, objections, and hesitations on these issues. Our meeting ultimately muddled through and learned many important lessons about loving and ministering to each other, about overcoming fear, anger, and divisiveness in the midst of very different visions of what being faithful on a particular moral issue might mean.

Greater spiritual clarity emerged over time through worship, listening, and dialogue in business meetings, as well as self-education efforts, such as a meeting-sponsored workshop on "Homophobia as a Spiritual Disease." By 1989, the meeting took its first marriage ceremony for a gay couple under its care, and this proved to be a joyous occasion. The process of exploring and being faithful to this aspect of the testimony of equality has continued. The meeting created a handout for newcomers expressing its commitment to be welcoming to all, has worked for change in the state marriage law and within the larger Society of Friends, and most recently has been supporting a couple in the meeting who legally married in Vermont, but who face the possibility of deportation of the immigrant spouse, since the federal government does not recognize their marriage.

I am pleased at how our meeting has grown spiritually and become ever more faithful to our testimony on equality as the years have gone by. Yet, it is important to remember that many members of our meeting did not always hold such faithful views and were once at ease with the conventional social prejudices against gays and lesbians in our meeting and in the wider society. We were helped in this transformation by those who were faithful and willing to struggle in love, who helped a new, "sensitive many" to rise in the meeting. We ended with a sense of unity and deeper faithfulness.

Today, I believe, a major challenge for Quakers striving to live more faithfully involves how we choose to conduct our relationship with our endangered planet and all those whose lives depend upon it. An increasing number of Quakers are urging the members of the Religious Society of Friends to let go of our culturally ingrained habits of consumerism, our dependency on convenience, and our reliance on sources of energy that deplete and poison the earth as we face the looming moral challenges of climate change, peak oil, and suffering caused by a dysfunctional global economy. As one example, a growing number of Quakers have come together since 1987 in the Quaker Earthcare Witness network. In many ways, and in many forums, these folks have invited Quakers to stop conforming to our unraveling industrial way of life and to respond instead with courage, creativity and positive visions for transitioning our societies toward a more resilient, simple, socially just, spiritually fulfilling, and ecologically sustainable world. I find this a very interesting time to be a Quaker. Mother Earth herself is crying out to us to help her and her children. What will we do?

We are still in the early stages of embracing this change in our lives. When I spoke at the Friendly Households Challenge launch in Philadelphia, I asked people to raise their hands if they believed that a significant percentage of the Quakers in their local meetings were still having trouble accepting the full implications of climate change, resource depletion, and global economic instability and injustice. Everyone in the room raised a hand.

I have been particularly inspired by the message of young Quakers who are part of my yearly meeting's Young Adult Friends Climate Working Group. Their 2011 report begins with a difficult truth, "Our lives are caught in a system/culture/society that exploits people and the planet, and leaves us spiritually wanting." After detailing their concerns, they raised a vision of the Beloved Community within our reach by saying, "We yearn for community that is intimately dependent on the earth, on our neighbors, and our own self-reliance to provide our basic needs, and allows us to see the consequences of our use of creation."

Like many others in my yearly meeting, I have been very moved by the witness of these young adult Quakers. For years, I too have been trying to move toward greater faithfulness along these lines—at home, at work, in my community, and as a citizen of my country and the world. One such opportunity that excites me is participation in the Transition movement, in which members of a local community work together to imagine and develop more resilient and sustainable local economies that meet local needs and serve local values and interests.

At the same yearly meeting gathering at which I spoke about healing a broken planet, I showed the film *Transition 1.0* one evening, and presented several interest groups with another transition organizer. I was delighted with the response. The bookstore sold 48 copies of *The Transition Handbook*, and the yearly meeting's earthcare ministries committee endorsed the idea of inviting all Quakers to consider joining the global Transition movement and they asked us to launch an online "Quakers In Transition" project to help equip Quakers to engage with their neighbors in positive local transition efforts. We have done so, and the response thus far has been very gratifying.

In the last several months, I've witnessed an increase in the number of requests from local Quaker meetings in New England for Transition talks, introductory workshops on "Transition, Faith, and Action," and the two-day training that Transition US provides for emerging local Transition organizers. It is hard to know how far this movement of loving our neighbors and God's good earth will go, but it feels possible to me that through this and other efforts, we may be moving toward some kind of tipping point among Quakers in the direction of greater faithfulness and inspired action in these challenging times.

Our journey toward faithfulness is often long, always challenging, sometimes painful, and sometimes ridiculously joyous. This is true for individuals, local meetings, and the Religious Society of Friends as a whole. This journey, in all its diversity and dimensions, is what makes a person a Quaker. Even just telling the truth, when you are tempted to lie to make yourself look good, is part of the journey towards faithfulness.

Anyway, I hope this letter helps you better understand some of our struggles to be faithful and also calms your worries about your not being "radical enough, or faithful enough to be a Quaker." In what ways have you moved into greater faithfulness over time? What have been your struggles and successes?

Affectionately,
Steve

LETTER 7

My Invitation to You

Dear Pat,

Great to hear from you again. I'm glad that my last letter reassured you about how Quakers try to be faithful and are, at the same time, quite ordinary people.

Now that you are attending meeting for worship fairly regularly and have gone to two monthly business meetings, you may well be hearing from your meeting's nominating committee within the year. They will likely ask if you would like to join a committee or take on some responsibility for the meeting. The nominating committee's charge is to match the needs of the meeting with the spiritual gifts and abilities of its members and regular attenders. I imagine that they will soon be exploring the possibilities with you, if you keep attending meeting in the coming months.

What, if anything, do you think you might be called to do to help your meeting thrive? This is worth thinking about. Because of my background in social activism and education, the Putney Friends Meeting's nominating committee originally thought my best contribution would be serving on the social justice and peace committee, as well as the adult religious education committee. I said yes to their requests. Yet, I soon discovered that this wasn't a good fit for me, too much like what I do in the world everyday. Still, I wanted to find a way to help out my new meeting and we kept in touch.

After serving on these two other committees for about a year, I ultimately proposed that I move off these two committees and instead create and maintain a meeting website that would help welcome and inform spiritual seekers and newcomers, as well as keep long-time members and attenders up to date on what is happening at our meeting. After a few discussions with members of nominating committee, we became clear that this likely was the best way for me to contribute to the meeting. I was relieved, of course, to lay down my two other committee responsibilities and take up this new challenge. The "fit" proved to be much better for both the meeting and me. Sometimes our best contributions are not as obvious as we think, but need a period of experimentation and discernment to identify clearly. Is any particular form of service tugging at you at this point? How do you see your gifts being used by your meeting?

Remember, too, you don't have to wait for the nominating committee to reach out to you first. You can also contact them and say you are increasingly feeling called to serve the meeting in some ongoing way besides regular attendance at meeting for worship. You can then discuss your strengths, interests, and sense of calling with some members of the nominating committee. If the members of your nominating committee are like ours, they will listen carefully, open this question to leadings of the Spirit, and work with you to find a good way forward, rather than just referring you to a work slot that needs to be filled. It is another way we minister one to another.

I do understand from your last letter that you are not yet clear about whether you "are here to stay for the long haul," but I appreciate your foresight in asking about what is involved in becoming a member of a Quaker meeting. For me, the basic shift happens prior to applying for membership. It happens whenever anyone has moved from being an experimental seeker exploring the Quaker way to becoming a regular attender and active participant within their new spiritual community.

In many meetings, very little distinction is made between official members and regular attenders. It is easy to feel fully included without going through the membership process. I chose not to become a formal member of the Galesburg or DeKalb Friends Meetings, but just acted, and was even accepted, as a full participant within these two spiritual communities. I was treated like a member because I regularly attended weekly meetings for worship and monthly business meetings, sought to live out the Quaker testimonies in my daily life, contributed money to the meeting, served on committees, and also worked to build ties of love and support with the other members and attenders of my meetings. In this capacity as an active participant, I had already found acceptance, shared values, personal transformation, and active participation in my spiritual community. I did not see how becoming a formal member would add to my spiritual life or to the well-being of my spiritual community. (You should know, however, that some meetings, especially if they are legally incorporated, may reserve a few particular appointments for formal members.)

For whatever reason, though, I felt very different after my spiritual re-awakening in my forties, when I once again returned to regular attendance and active participation in a Quaker meeting. I now felt an inner pull to make my commitment clear and public, to be more open to questions and guidance from others, and to explore and test my leading to return to the Quaker way with seasoned members from my new meeting. Applying for membership in a Quaker meeting is not at all like joining the Sierra Club. You don't just sign a form and send in your dues. You engage instead in an open, unrushed, and mutual discernment process with other members of the meeting to see if this next step makes sense. I found myself wanting to experience this spiritual rite of passage, and I also felt it might lead to an even sounder relationship with the Quaker movement than I had known as a teenager and young adult.

In my yearly meeting's book of *Faith and Practice*, it says that the "appropriate time to apply for membership will vary from person to person," but one vitally important indicator "that the time to apply may be approaching is the recognition that meeting for worship has become a central part of one's life." Another indicator is when you start feeling ready "to enter wholeheartedly into the spiritual and corporate activities of the Society and to assume responsibility for both service and support, as way opens." This Quaker guidebook also suggests that you can prepare yourself to apply for membership "by careful reading of this book of *Faith and Practice*, by discussion with meeting members, and by study of the literature interpreting Friends' beliefs." I only applied for membership at Putney Friends Meeting after all three of these things were true for me.

So, what is the process? It varies a little from meeting to meeting and is outlined in each yearly meeting's *Faith and Practice*, which is probably on a shelf in the library of the meeting you are attending. At Putney Friends Meeting, I started by writing a letter to the meeting's clerk requesting membership. The meeting's membership pamphlet explains that "the letter should relate why the applicant wishes to become a member and may give a picture of his or her spiritual history, sense of unity with the beliefs and practices of Friends, and of her or his sense of belonging to the Putney Friend's spiritual community." I found it a lovely and meaningful process to reflect deeply about my past spiritual life and my future vision as I crafted and re-crafted my letter before sending it in.

The clerk of the meeting passes the letter on to our ministry and counsel committee. (The responsible committee may have a different name in the meeting you are attending.) That committee appoints a few members of the meeting to serve on what is called a "clearness committee." In my case, the clearness committee met with me three times for a good hour or two each time, although it's pretty common for there to be only one or two such meetings. The goals of these meetings were to get to know each other better and mutually discern whether we were in fact clear about the appropriateness, for both me and the meeting, to take this next step in our relationship together. As the Putney membership information pamphlet notes, in these discussions, the "emphasis will be on the fact that becoming a Friend is a relatively simple procedure, while being a friend is a lifetime process."

The clearness committee ultimately reports on the nature of its discussion with the applicant and that report makes its way back to monthly meeting for business. I found that meeting for business particularly meaningful. A member of my clearness committee gave a summary of the committee's experience of talking with me. Another member of the committee read an extract from my letter of application and then those present at the meeting expressed joy and appreciation. The clerk tested the "sense of the meeting" by preparing and reading out a minute formalizing my membership. I then was able to thank everyone and speak briefly about what this means to me and how I looked forward to my role as a member of the meeting. It was lovely, low key, and moving.

While I was delighted with the outcome, I also loved the process of meeting with my clearness committee. I found significant value in those thoughtful back-and-forth discussions. Not only did the committee ask me interesting questions, they were also direct with me about any concerns they had. At least one member of my committee was concerned that I might be a very orthodox Christian and therefore unable to embrace the theological diversity that was in the room during our meetings for worship. We talked this through and resolved this issue to everyone's satisfaction.

They also took the time to answer my questions. Mostly, though, I just related some of the highlights (and lowlights) of my spiritual journey among Quakers and outside of the Quaker movement. We then had an in-depth discussion of the ins and outs of several points of Quaker faith and practice, as each of us understood them. I particularly remember talking candidly about a concern I had. I explained that from my past experience with Quakers and all the study I had done, I was honestly able to say that I was in profound unity with Quaker principles and testimonies with the possible exception of one: the Quaker peace testimony.

Quakers are one of the three historic "peace churches" that have adopted an uncompromising stand against international war and seek to love our enemies, be peacemakers, and find nonviolent solutions to conflicts within our local and world communities. As Quakers, we take the sermon on the mount seriously, treasure "that of God" in everyone, and promote a nonviolent path to the Beloved Community. We feel called by the divine Spirit to maximize love and justice in the world and, as my book of *Faith and Practice* puts it, to "root out the causes of war from our lives and from the political and social structures about us." I have no problem with any of this. In fact, these core convictions are a huge part of why I have always been attracted to the Quaker way.

Yet, as a teenager, I interpreted the Quaker peace testimony as being a commitment to absolute pacifism. At the time, I even rather judgmentally argued that anyone who engaged in either personal or political violence, no matter what the reason or outcome, was lost in sin. Back then, I could not think of a single instance or circumstance where a violent response to a situation might be God's will, or close to it. This absolute rejection of violence and physical force, no matter what the situation or context, seemed like a defining feature of the Quaker peace testimony to me. If this were actually true, I thought it might not make sense for me to become a member of a Quaker meeting.

I told my clearness committee about the moment when I lost my commitment to absolute pacifism. I was in my early twenties and standing in line with my wife waiting to get an ice cream cone at a shopping center. All of a sudden, just a little ahead of us in the line, I saw a white man start to yell at and then physically attack a black guy standing in front of him. I was stunned and shocked, but I felt I had to act.

In that split second, however, I could not think of any non-violent way to intervene, as I had recently done in downtown Minneapolis when a drunk man was yelling and hitting a woman on the street. That man had been slow, stumbled a bit, and sometimes stepped back away from the woman, who had fallen to the ground. In that particular situation, I just put myself between the woman and the man. He hit me several times, sometimes even pretty hard, but I had no trouble just taking the punches and slowly talking this guy down and finally getting him to go home. I was then able to help the woman collect herself and get to a safe place.

Yet, this time at the shopping center was different. The attacker was stone sober, apparently had no ongoing emotional relationship with his victim, and was grabbing the other guy and choking and punching him at close range. I saw no way to get between the two men and take the punches until the attacker could calm down. People around the attacker were already urging him to stop hitting the other guy, and the attacker was paying no attention to them. What to do? I couldn't just let him keep punching and choking the other man, so I walked up behind the attacker, put him in a full nelson wrestling hold, and then kicked out his legs from under him and pushed the man down fast so his knees would hit the stone floor hard and it would hurt him enough that he wouldn't want or be able to jump back up and keep fighting.

Much to my surprise, this strategic use of limited violence worked. He didn't get up off the floor. I kept holding him as gently as possible, said I was sorry to have had to grab him, but that he really had to stop attacking the other man. I also told him I would make sure that he wasn't attacked in retaliation, but that I wasn't going to let him get up until he calmed down and agreed to stop fighting and go home. Eventually, a security guard walked up to us, asked me to move away from the man, took everyone's statements, told me I could go, and then escorted the attacker off the premises.

My wife and I found a distant hallway in the shopping center where we could be alone and I fell on the floor crying and shaking while she held me. Part of this outburst was the release of my own pent-up fear, but mostly I was crying uncontrollably because I felt I had violated everything I held sacred about the peace testimony, and this broke my heart. My world of uncomplicated, absolute pacifism crumbled that day and has never fully recovered. I could now see the value, in some circumstances, of limited, defensive violence when it is engaged in without vengeance or a desire for retaliation and when a viable nonviolent alternative to resist evil and aggression does not seem to be at hand.

Since that fateful day, I have come to embrace the nonviolent revolutionary approach hinted at by Jesus and fully embodied by Gandhi. Gandhi, for example, opposed any notion of "pacifism" that would be content with accepting social evils and avoiding the struggle for justice. He said it is better to resist social evil violently than not at all. This approach put him at odds with many religious pacifists. However, Gandhi also said that it is far better to discover and develop nonviolent ways to resist evil and support justice than to engage in violence, which is always tragic, often counter-productive, and frequently open to the temptation of descending into hatred and demonization of one's enemies. I agree with him on this too.

My question to my clearness committee was, "Do Quakers have to be absolute pacifists or can our spiritual community also embrace people committed to a non-pacifist, Gandhian approach to nonviolence?" This sparked deep discussion and soul searching among us. The members of my committee began their response by saying that they appreciated my candor, my deep reflection on the subject, and the many ways I was obviously in unity with the Quaker peace testimony. One committee member pointed out that many Quakers have made a distinction between international war with indiscriminate weapons of mass destruction and the well-targeted and strategic use of limited violence by domestic police forces in defending the rights and safety of the wider community. The members of my committee also felt comfortable with my level of unity with the Quaker peace testimony.

I've now been a member of Putney Friends Meeting for over six years and this clear mutual commitment, and the thoughtful process that led up to it, has meant so much to me. I'm not sure if I would have ever had this deep and candid conversation about nonviolence with members of my meeting without the context of our clearness committee membership discussions. This is just some of the value that I see in going through this process.

Now, before I close this letter, I want to make a specific invitation to you. If it ever begins to feel right for you to explore membership in a Quaker meeting, I hope you will feel encouraged and welcomed to embark on this process. New England Yearly Meeting's *Faith and Practice* clearly says, "The Society should reach out to and welcome into active membership all who find unity with the principles and the testimonies of Friends." Still, offering this kind of invitation to active and regular attenders sometimes seems hard for many meetings to do. Many Quakers feel like they are intruding, or proselytizing, or sending a message that the active participation of a regular attender is not good enough if they invite someone to consider applying to be a member of the meeting. So they often just wait patiently for the attender to request membership.

I just got an email from a Quaker I know in Philadelphia. In her note, she wrote, "I know of one longtime attender who felt let down and rejected by the meeting she had attended because over the course of a dozen years or so, they never invited her to join!" This sometimes happens. If it happens to you at the meeting you attend, please know that the members of that meeting will actually be thrilled to explore your becoming a member if you are led to take that step. This is true even if they don't mention it to you ahead of time.

Please take this letter as your invitation to worship with and perhaps join the Quaker movement if you come to believe that this is the right next step in your spiritual journey, as I ultimately decided it was in mine.

Affectionately,
Steve

P.S. I'm very glad you are thinking about coming to the Friends General Conference Gathering this summer. I am planning on going myself and I would love to spend a week with you in a temporary village of over 1,000 Quakers seeking truth, spiritual growth, fun, good food, and a little dancing. Let me know!

APPENDIX I

Advices and Queries

AUTHOR'S NOTE: Each Yearly Meeting adopts its own book of faith and practice (sometimes called a discipline). So, while often similar in overall tone, each Yearly Meeting's agreed upon set of "Advices and Queries" is different. Below are the Advices and Queries from the 1985 edition of the *Faith and Practice of the New England Yearly Meeting of Friends*. A revised version of this *Faith and Practice* book for New England is being worked on, but it was not finalized and fully approved by the time this book was published. I hope you find these Advices and Queries useful in your continuing effort to learn more about the Quaker movement.

The Advices

The Advices have served Friends for many generations in their search for a life centered in the Spirit. Arising from the experience and aspirations of successive generations of Friends, the Advices are illustrations of how they seek to carry their faith into all aspects of life.

Advices first appeared in the form of epistles sent among Friends to encourage and strengthen each other in their faith. The earliest surviving collection of Advices was issued from Balby in England in 1656. Its concluding statement begins, "Dearly beloved Friends, these things we do not lay upon you as a rule or form to walk by . . ."

Friends find their essential unity in their profound and exhilarating belief in the pervasive presence of God and in the continuing responsibility of each person and worshipping group to seek the leading of the Spirit in all things. Obedience to the leading of that Spirit rather than to any written statement of belief or conduct is the obligation of their faith.

Yet the Advices should have a quickening influence in shaping our daily lives. Their reading is intended to remind us that all aspects of our lives are under divine guidance and to heighten our awareness that in all our relationships we act in the sight of God.

Spiritual Life

Take heed, dear Friends, to the promptings of love and truth in your hearts, which are the leadings of the Holy Spirit. It is God's redemptive love that draws us, a love shown forth by Jesus in all his life, on the cross, and in his abiding presence.

Friends are advised to make a quiet place in their daily lives for prayer and communion with God and to be constant in the reading of the Bible and other devotional literature.

Let us cherish the seed of God in ourselves and in others, that we may be open to new revelations of truth. Let us look to our meetings to guide and stimulate our spiritual growth.

Meeting for Worship

Consider with care how God reaches us in meeting for worship. To every Friend is given a share of responsibility for the meeting. Friends are advised, therefore, to be diligent in attendance at meetings and in inward preparation for them. Let us be concerned to enter reverently into communion with God and with one another, to yield ourselves to the influence of the divine presence. Then what is evil in us may be weakened and the good raised up. God calls each one to the service of the meeting; let us be obedient and faithful, whether by word, by song, or by silent waiting, and let us receive the messages of others in a tender spirit.

Meeting Business

In meetings for business, and in all duties connected with them, seek again the leadings of the Light; let our utterances be brief and without repetition. Let us keep from obstinacy and from harshness of tone or manner and admit the possibility of being in error. In all the affairs of the meeting community, let us proceed in a peaceable spirit, with forbearance and warm affection for each other.

The Meeting Community

Let us live in love as members of a Christian community. Let us be ready to give and receive help, to rejoice together in the blessings of life and to sympathize with each other in its trials.

Let us maintain unity: let us avoid tale-bearing and detraction, acknowledge differences and seek to settle conflicts promptly in a manner free from resentment and all forms of inward violence; let us visit one another, making sure that those who are alone are drawn into the wider family of Friends. Thus, we may know one another as fellow workers in the things that endure.

Outreach

The power of God is not used to compel us to Truth; therefore, let us renounce for ourselves the power of any person over any other and, compelling no one, let us seek to lead others to Truth through love. Let us teach by being ourselves teachable.

Friends are advised to witness to the power of Truth and justice and to foster growth of the divine community at home and abroad. While remaining faithful to our Quaker insights, and ready to share them with others, let us seek to understand the contributions made by the people of God everywhere. Whenever possible, let us seek to enter into prayer and work with the wider community of faith.

Personal Conduct

Let us bring the whole of our daily lives under the ordering of the Spirit. Let our faith free us from crippling fears so that we may live adventurously. In relations with others, let us exercise imagination, understanding, and sympathy. Let us live and work in the plainness and simplicity of true followers of Christ.

In view of the evils arising from the use of tobacco and intoxicating drinks and from the abuse of drugs, Friends are advised to consider whether they should refrain from using them, from offering them to others, and from having any share in their manufacture or sale. We should not let the claims of good fellowship or the fear of seeming peculiar influence our decision.

Let us maintain integrity in word and deed. Holding to the simplicity of truth, let us keep free of oaths. Remember how widespread and diverse are the temptations to grow rich at the expense of others, and how apparently harmless indulgence often leads by degrees to wrong-doing. Let us avoid and discourage every kind of betting and gambling and commercial speculations of a gambling character.

Friends have always held that the sacred nature of a sexual relationship is affirmed only in marriage. In recent times, however, some Friends have found such affirmation in other contexts. Let us be certain, in any case, that we hold up to the Light any sexual relationship we may be considering and reject any relationship that may violate the integrity or spiritual welfare of either of the partners or of others. No relationship can be a right one which makes use of another person through selfish desire.

Home and Family

Let your lives benefit from the power of friendship and the solace of solitude. Rejoice in the beauty of those friendships which grow in depth, understanding, and mutual respect.

Friends are advised to seek divine guidance when considering marriage and to enter marriage with a commitment to cherish each other for life. In marriage, treasure the joys of intimacy, share the sorrows of losses, and mediate differences with patience. Be ready to seek the counsel of your own parents or of other experienced persons as it is needed. Consider together the responsibilities of parenthood.

Let us trust in the Light and witness to it in our daily living. We and our families are children of God with a rich accessible record of God's dealings with humanity. In dress, in furnishings, in manners, in diet, and in entertainment, let us choose the simple, the wholesome, and the beautiful. Let us be cooperative and creative in family recreation so that it encourages mutual activity and sharing.

Let us dwell with thankfulness on the blessings and happiness that life has brought us. Friends are advised to try throughout life to discern the appropriate moment to relinquish responsibilities to others. Let us face with courage the approach of old age, both for ourselves and for those dear to us, realizing that even as our outward activity lessens, our seasoned thought and prayer may liberate love and power in others.

Friends are advised to make provision for the settlement of their affairs while in health so that others may not be burdened. Such provision may include maintaining an up-to-date will and discussing with family and doctors our wishes in the event of serious illness or death.

Care of Children

Care of the children of the meeting should be the responsibility of every Friend. Let us share with our children a sense of adventure, of wonder, and of trust and let them know that, in facing the mysteries of life, they are surrounded by love. Both parents and meetings need to guard against letting other commitments deprive children of the time and attention they need.

Friends are advised to seek for children the full development of God's gifts, which is true education. All Friends are cautioned against harshness of tone or manner when offering counsel or reproof. To the child, even a seeming harshness may check the beginnings of repentance or growth, and a lack of sympathy may cause harm where only good was intended. Let us nurture a spirit of common concern, thereby giving children a sense of belonging to a larger community.

Stewardship

Friends are advised to consider our possessions as God's gifts, entrusted to us for responsible use. Let us free our time and our abilities to be able to follow the leadings of the Spirit. Let us cherish the beauty and variety of the world. Friends are urged to speak out boldly against the destruction of the world's resources and the difficulties that destruction prepares for the future generations. Let us guard against waste and resist our extravagant consumption, which contributes to inequities and impoverishment of life in our own and other societies. Let us show a loving consideration for all God's creatures. Let kindness know no limits.

Vocations

In our relations with others in our daily work, let us manifest the spirit of justice and understanding and thus give a living witness to the Truth. While trying to make provision for ourselves and our families, let us not be anxious, but in quietness of spirit trust in the goodness of God. When we suffer from unemployment, let us seek the support and encouragement of our meetings. When we have a choice of employment, let us think first of the service that we may render. Let us be ready to limit our engagements, to withdraw for a time, or even to retire from a business that we may be free for new service as God appoints it.

Social Responsibility

Friends are called, as followers of Christ, to help establish the Kingdom of God on earth. Let us strengthen a sense of kinship with everyone. Let that sense of kinship inspire us in our efforts to build a social order free of violence and oppression, in which no person's development is thwarted by poverty and the lack of health care, education, or freedom. Friends are advised to minister to those in need but also to seek to know the facts and the causes of social and economic ills and to work for the removal of those ills. Let us cherish every human being and encourage efforts to overcome all forms of prejudice.

Peace and Reconciliation

Every human being is a child of God with a measure of God's Light. War and other instruments of violence and oppression ignore this reality and violate our relation with God. Let us keep primary, therefore, Friends' concern for removing the causes of war. Let us seek, through God's power and grace, to overcome in our own hearts the emotions that lie at the root of violence. At every opportunity, let us be peacemakers in our homes, in our communities, and in our places of work. Let us take care that we who declare against war do not nourish the seeds of war in our possessions. Friends are urged to support those who witness to their governments and take personal risks in the cause of peace, who choose not to participate in war as soldiers nor to contribute to its preparations with their taxes. Let us support in all possible ways the development of international order, justice, and understanding.

Finally, dear Friends, let us follow steadfastly after all that is pure and lovely and of good report. Let us be prayerful, be watchful, be humble. Let not failure discourage us. Let our whole conduct and conversation be worthy of disciples of Christ.

The Queries

Friends have developed the Queries to assist us to consider prayerfully the true source of spiritual strength and the extent to which the conduct of our lives gives witness to our Christian faith. To these ends, the Queries should be read frequently in private devotions and regularly in monthly and quarterly meetings.

In using these Queries, meetings should be aware that our standards of conduct do not derive from an outward set of rules but rather from the life and teachings of Jesus as recorded in the New Testament, from the examples offered by the spiritual experiences and lives of those who have preceded us, and from our own encounters with that inward revelation through which "the way, the truth, and the life" seek expression today.

1. Spiritual Life

○ Do you live in thankful awareness of God's constant presence in your life?

○ Are you sensitive and obedient to leadings of the Holy Spirit?

○ Do you seek to follow Jesus, who shows us the way?

○ Do you nurture your spiritual life with prayer and silent waiting and with regular study of the Bible and other devotional literature?

2. Meeting for Worship

○ Are meetings for worship held in expectant waiting for divine guidance?

○ Are you faithful and punctual in attendance?

○ Do you come in a spirit of openness with heart and mind prepared for communion with God?

○ Do both silent and vocal ministry arise in response to the leading of the Holy Spirit?

○ Do all other activities of your meeting find their inspiration in worship, and do they, in turn, help to uphold the worshipping group?

3. Meeting Business

○ Are meetings for business held in a spirit of worship and prayerful search for the way of Truth?

○ Are all members encouraged to use their talents in the service of the meeting?

○ Do you undertake your proper share of the work and financial support of the meeting?

4. The Meeting Community

○ Do you love one another as becomes the followers of Christ? Do you share each other's joys and burdens?

○ When conflicts arise, do you seek in mutual forgiveness and tenderness to resolve them speedily?

○ Are you careful of the reputation of others? Do you seek beyond all differences of opinion and circumstance for unity in the divine life?

5. Outreach

○ Do you welcome inquirers and visitors to your meeting?

○ Do you encourage their continued attendance and participation?

○ Do you seek to share and to interpret the faith of Friends and to cooperate with others in spreading the Christian message?

○ Are you patterns, examples; do your lives preach among all sorts of people, and to them?

○ Do you walk cheerfully over the world, answering that of God in every one?

6. Personal Conduct

○ Do you live with simplicity, moderation, and integrity?

○ Are you punctual in keeping promises, careful in speech, just and compassionate in all your dealings with others?

○ Do you take care that your spiritual growth is not sacrificed to busyness but instead integrates your life's activities?

○ Are your recreations consistent with Quaker values; do they refresh your spirit and renew your body and mind?

7. Home and Family

○ Do you make your home a place of friendliness, refreshment, and peace, where God becomes more real to those who live there and to all who visit there?

○ Is worship a daily part of your personal and family life?

○ Do you recognize marriage as a sacred, loving, and permanent relationship requiring mutual consideration and adjustments?

○ Should conflict or crisis threaten the stability of the home, are you open to seeking all necessary help, both from your meeting and from the larger community?

8. Care of Children

○ Do children receive the loving care of your meeting?

○ Does the meeting nurture their religious life and give them an understanding of the principles and practices of Friends?

○ Are you an example to your children in your faithfulness to the ideals you profess?

○ Do you promote your children's moral and spiritual development by loving oversight of their education, recreation, and social activities?

○ Do you listen to children, recognizing that the Spirit may lead them along paths you have not foreseen? Do you assist them to assume their rightful responsibilities in the home, the meeting, and the community?

9. Stewardship

○ Do you revere all life and the splendor of God's continuing creation?

○ Do you try to protect the natural environment and its creatures against abuse and harmful exploitation?

○ Do you regard your possessions as given to you in trust, and do you part with them freely to meet the needs of others?

○ Are you frugal in your personal life and committed to the just distribution of the world's resources?

10. Vocations

○ Do you respect the value of all useful work, whether paid or unpaid, whether physical or intellectual, whether performed in the home or in the larger community?

○ Does your daily work use means and serve goals which are consistent with the teachings of Jesus?

○ Are you honest and trustworthy in all business transactions, prompt and just in payment of debts?

○ By counsel and example, do you encourage young people to enter vocations which will serve society?

11. Social Responsibility

○ Do you respect the worth of every human being as a child of God?

○ Do you uphold the right of all persons to justice and human dignity?

- ○ Do you endeavor to create political, social, and economic institutions which will sustain and enrich the life of all?
- ○ Do you fulfill all civic obligations which are not contrary to divine leadings?
- ○ Do you give spiritual and material support to those who suffer for conscience's sake?

12. Peace and Reconciliation

- ○ Do you "live in the virtue of that life and power that takes away the occasion of all wars"?
- ○ Do you faithfully maintain Friends' testimony against military preparations and all participation in war, as inconsistent with the teachings and spirit of Christ?
- ○ Do you strive to increase understanding and use of non-violent methods of resolving conflicts?
- ○ Do you take your part in the ministry of reconciliation between individuals, groups, and nations?
- ○ When discouraged, do you remember that Jesus said, "Peace is my parting gift to you, my own peace, such the world cannot give. Set your troubled hearts at rest, and banish your fears"? John 14:27 NEB

APPENDIX II
Additional Resources

I. Works Quoted or Mentioned in the Letters
  (in order of appearance)

Faith and Practice of New England Yearly Meeting of Friends (New England Yearly Meeting of Friends, 1985).

Barclay's Apology In Modern English, by Robert Barclay and edited by Dean Freiday (Barclay Press, 1991).

The Journal of George Fox, a revised edition by John L. Nickalls (Quaker Books, 2005).

The Green Bible: Understanding the Bible's Powerful Message for the Earth, the New Revised Standard Version, foreword by Desmond Tutu (Harper One, 2008).

Declaration of Samuel D. Caldwell in "Declarations and Exhibits in Support of Defendant's Motion for Summary Judgment." United States of America v. Philadelphia Yearly Meeting of the Religious Society of Friends, U.S. District Court, Eastern District of Pennsylvania, Civil Nos. 88-6368 and 88-6390, March 31, 1989.

If the Church Were Christian: Rediscovering the Values of Jesus, by Philip Gulley (Harper One, 2010).

To Be Broken and Tender: A Quaker Theology for Today, by Margery Post Abbott (Friends Bulletin Corporation, 2010).

Listening to the Light: How to Bring Quaker Simplicity and Integrity into Our Lives, by Jim Pym (Rider, 1999).

Blessed Are The Organized: How Quakers Can Help Their Local Communities Transition From Oil Dependency To A Simpler, Just, and More Resilient Way of Life, the Sunday plenary talk delivered by

Steve Chase at the August, 2011, Annual Sessions of New England Yearly Meeting of Friends (neym.org/recordings/2011/NEYM-2011-Steve-Chase.mp3).

Strength To Love, by Martin Luther King, Jr. (Fortress Press; Gift edition, 2010).

Fit for Freedom, Not for Friendship: Quakers, African Americans, and the Myth of Racial Justice, by Donna McDaniel and Vanessa Julye (Quaker Press, 2009).

Spiritual Discernment: The Context and Goal of Clearness Committees, by Patricia Loring (Pendle Hill Pamphlet Series, 1992).

January 2011 Report of the Young Adult Friends Climate Working Group (www.neym.org/mid-year/YAF-Climate-Report.html).

The Transition Handbook: From Oil Dependence to Local Resilience, by Rob Hopkins (Chelsea Green, 2008).

In Transition 1.0, a 50 minute 2009 documentary created by the international Transition Network (vimeo.com/groups/22864/videos/8029815).

Quakers In Transition: An online project of New England Yearly Meeting's Earthcare Witness Committee (quakersintransition.wordpress.com/).

Membership in the Religious Society of Friends at Putney Friends Meeting, New England Yearly Meeting (Putney Friends, nd.).

II. Books Recommended for Seekers and Newcomers

Being A Quaker: A Guide for Newcomers, by Georffrey Durham (Quaker Quest, 2011).

Holy Silence: The Gift of Quaker Spirituality, by J. Brent Bill (Paraclete Press, 2005).

Silence and Witness: The Quaker Tradition, by Michael L. Birkel (Orbis Books, 2004).

Listening Spirituality I: Personal Spiritual Practices Among Friends, by Patricia Loring (Opening Press, 1997).

Listening Spirituality II: Corporate Spiritual Practice Among Friends, by Patricia Loring (Opening Press, 1999).

Quakerism: A Theology for Our Time, by Patricia Williams (Infinity Publishing, 2008).

New Light: 12 Quaker Voices, edited by Jennifer Kavanagh (O Books, 2008).

Spirit Rising: Young Quaker Voices, edited Angelina Conti, et al. (Quaker Press, 2010).

Black Fire: African American Quakers on Spirituality and Human Rights, edited by Harold Weaver, Jr., et al. (Quaker Press, 2011).

III. Quaker Periodicals

Friends Journal is published monthly by the Friends Publishing Corporation, and its mission is to serve the Quaker community and the wider community of spiritual seekers through the publication of articles, poetry, letters, art, and news that convey the contemporary Quaker life and thought. Check them out on the web at www.friendsjournal.org/.

Quaker Life magazine is published by Friends United Meeting six times a year. Regular features include a Bible study column, stories of God's transforming presence in Friend's lives, news from around the Quaker world as well as stories of FUM ministries, reader's essays, reviews, classified advertising, a meeting directory, and, of course, letters to the editor. Check them out on the web at www.fum.org/QL/.

Befriending Creation is a bi-monthly newsletter publish by Quaker Earthcare Witness. It reports and celebrates what Friends and Friends Meetings and organizations are doing and saying about the global crisis in ecological sustainability. Its mission is to promote Quaker Earthcare Witness goals, stimulate discussion and action, share insights, practical ideas, and news of our actions, and encourage among Friends a sense of community and spiritual connection with all Creation. Check them out on the web at www.quakerearthcare.org/Publications/BeFriendingCreation/Pub-AboutBFC.html.

IV. Quaker Organizations I Belong To

Putney Friends Meeting
www.putneyfriends.wordpress.com/

New England Yearly Meeting
www.neym.org/

Friends General Conference
www.fgcquaker.org/

Friends United Meeting
www.fum.org/

V. Other Useful Websites

Quaker Information Center
www.quakerinfo.org/

QuakerBooks of FGC (an online bookstore)
www.quakerbooks.org/

Online Yearly Meeting Books of *Faith and Practice*
www.quakerinfo.org/quakerism/faithandpractice

Online Directory of Quaker Meetings
www.quakerfinder.org/

An Online Portal to Quaker Blogs
www.quakerquaker.org/

VI. Quaker Conference Centers

Those new to Quakers often profit from and enjoy introductory courses at Quaker conference centers. Here's a list:

Ben Lomond Quaker Center
(Pacific Yearly Meeting)
P.O. Box 686
Ben Lomond, CA 95005
Web: www.quakercenter.org
Email: mail@quakercenter.org
Phone: (831) 336-8333

Pendle Hill
338 Plush Mill Road
Wallingford, PA 10986
Web: www.pendlehill.org
Email: pendlehill@pendlehill.org
Phone: (800) 742-3150

Powell House
(New York Yearly Meeting)
524 Pitt Hall Road
Old Chatham, NY 12136
Web: www.powellhouse.org
Email: powellhse@aol.com
Phone: (518) 794-8811

William Penn House
515 East Capitol St., SE
Washington, D.C. 20003
Phone: (202) 543-0445
Web: williampennhouse.org/
Email: dirpennhouse@pennsnet.org

Woolman Hill
(New England Yearly Meeting)
107 Keats Road
Deerfield, MA 01342
Web: www.woolmanhill.org
Email: info@woolmanhill.org
Phone: (413) 774-3431

APPENDIX III

About the Author

Steve Chase lives in Keene, New Hampshire, and is a member of Putney Friends Meeting and the New England Yearly Meeting of Friends. He is a frequent writer for *Friends Journal* and has also written for *Quaker Life*. He serves on the national Quaker Quest Traveling Team of Friends General Conference and has led workshops on various topics at Quaker retreat centers such as Pendle Hill in Pennsylvania and Woolman Hill in Massachusetts. He has also co-led workshops at the annual sessions of New England Yearly Meeting and at Friends General Conference gatherings. He and his wife Katy Locke also co-facilitate Awakening the Dreamer workshops for Quaker meetings and gatherings as well as schools, community groups, and other faith communities.

Steve is the educational director of Antioch University New England's Environmental Studies master's program in Advocacy in Social Justice and Sustainability, and one of the co-founders of the Transition Keene Task Force, the 56th Transition Initiative in the United States and the first in New Hampshire. He is also the co-director of the online *Quakers in Transition* project sponsored by New England Yearly Meeting's Earthcare Ministries Committee, and he gave the keynote address at the New England Yearly Meeting annual summer sessions in 2011. His talk was entitled *Blessed Are The Organized: How Quakers Can Help Their Local Communities Transition From Oil Dependency To A Simpler, Just, and More Resilient Way of Life*. He and his wife Katy also offer day-long and weekend workshops entitled *Transition, Faith, and Action: An Interactive Introduction to the Transition Movement for People of Faith.*

Steve's writing of this book and his traveling ministry among Friends and other spiritual communities is under the oversight of a committee set up by Putney Friends Meeting. Below is Putney Friends Meeting's letter of support for Steve's ministry.

Dear Friends in New England Yearly Meeting and beyond,

We at Putney Friends Meeting are writing in support of the traveling ministry of Steve Chase. Steve is a treasured member of Putney Friends Meeting who has long shared a gift for prophetic and soulful ministry in our Meetings for Worship. He is increasingly called to share his ministry with Friends and others. Whether through his writing, speaking, or leading workshops or retreats, we can attest that Steve's work in the traveling ministry is deeply rooted in 1) loving God with all one's heart, soul, and strength; 2) loving our neighbors as ourselves; and 3) loving God's good earth by acting in unity with Creation.

We trust you will welcome Steve into your community, show him every hospitality, care for his spiritual life while he is among you, and hope that you will be uplifted by his ministry in whatever form it takes.

Sincerely,
Carol Forsythe, Clerk of Putney Friends Meeting

APPENDIX IV
Acknowledgements

In the fourth letter in this book, I quote my friend Noah Baker Merrill saying, "It takes a meeting to raise a ministry." In my case, it has taken several meetings. This book would not exist without the love, support, and challenges from the Quakers I've known at Galesburg, DeKalb, Keene, and Putney Friends Meetings, where I've been a regular attender or a member, as well as the Twin Cities and Cambridge Friends Meetings, where I dabbled a bit during my "interlude away" from the Religious Society of Friends. I am also especially grateful to George Lakey, a traveling minister from Central Philadelphia Monthly Meeting who has been a Quaker mentor of mine since I was fifteen. He has long encouraged me spiritually as a Quaker dad, writer, activist, and educator.

Two staff members from Friends General Conference, Elaine Crauderueff, Ministries & Quaker Quest Coordinator, and Chel Avery, Communications & Publications Coordinator, are perhaps the most responsible for this book being written. They invited me to write it, had faith in me when I missed a deadline or two, and read and commented in detail on all the various drafts of this manuscript. Chel, in particular, provided me with expert guidance as both my editor and publisher in her role as the head of QuakerPress. Few writers have ever been in such capable hands.

At Putney Friends Meeting, I particularly want to thank Parker Huber, Carol Forsythe, Roger Vincent Jasaitis, and Eva Mondon of my Ministry Oversight Committee for reading drafts of this book and sharing their insightful feedback with me. The book is much improved because of their efforts. Other Friends and friends have also read and commented on different drafts, including Chris Andres, Sue Gentile, Mark Jensen, and Carol Packwood.

I also want to thank Katy Locke, my beloved life partner of seventeen years. She let me talk out loud about the evolving manuscript on our regular walks around the pond at Robin Hood Park and she read the entire manuscript a couple of times and pointed out the places that made her laugh, moved her, sparked an "aha" moment, or confused her. I worked hard at clarifying all the confusing parts, which might well have escaped me without her thoughtful feedback.

Finally, I dedicate this book to my mother, Sue Chase. As it says in the fifth letter, she was my first spiritual teacher and she remains an important one for me to this day.

CPSIA information can be obtained at www.ICGtesting.com
Printed in the USA
LVOW05s1804201113

362115LV00005B/563/P